ELDERS

THE BIBLICAL QUALIFICATIONS OF CHURCH ELDERS

Larry Nelson

This book is self-published by Larry Nelson of Christian Family Services.

Text copyright © 2020 Larry Nelson

All rights reserved for the intellectual content of this work. No part of this book may be reproduced in any form or by any means without the express written consent of the author, Larry Nelson, or Christian Family Services.

Christian Family Services
701 Arthurs Way
Sumas, WA 98295

Cover design: Mario Richard
Cover image: Iren Moroz, Shutterstock.com

ISBN-13: 978-0-578-78524-0

First Edition: November 2020

DEDICATION

To my beloved wife, Marian,
who has loved and encouraged me throughout
almost 50 years of marriage and ministry together,
and without whom this book could never
have been written.

Her children rise up and bless her;
Her husband also, and he praises her, saying:
"Many daughters have done nobly,
But you excel them all."
(Proverbs 31:28-29)

FOREWORD

"Who can calculate the damage done during the past 2000 years to the churches of Jesus Christ because of inattentive, naïve, and prayerless shepherds? Many churches and denominations that once stood for sound, orthodox doctrine and life now reject every major tenet of the Christian faith and condone the most deplorable moral practices conceivable. How did this happen? The local church leaders were naïve, untaught, and prayerless and became inattentive to Satan's deceptive strategies. They were blind watchmen and dumb dogs, preoccupied with their own self-interest and comforts. When their seminaries jettisoned the truth of the gospel and the divine inspiration of the Bible, they were asleep. They naïvely invited young wolves in sheep's clothing into their flocks to be their spiritual shepherds. Hence they and their flocks have been devoured by wolves." [1]

- Alexander Strauch

The Lord Jesus Christ cares about the leadership of His church. He shed His blood to purchase His people from the slave market of sin (Acts 20:28) and to secure their salvation everlastingly (John 10:14-18, 25-30). The Lord of the Church is committed to the holiness of His people (Ephesians 5:25-30). He has given instructions through His apostles for the

---

[1] Alexander Strauch, *Biblical Eldership: An Urgent Call to Restore Biblical Church Leadership* (Littleton: Lewis and Roth Publishers, 1995), 20.

administration, leadership, training, discipleship, and structure of His church. Sadly, the will of the Lord Jesus Christ concerning the affairs of His church is often ignored.

The importance of leadership in this precious, holy, blood-bought institution cannot be overstated. For generations, most of the church in North America has ignored the biblical instructions for church structure and leadership qualifications. The result has been a widespread ignorance of, and disobedience to, the Lord's clear commands.

The only way to reverse this diseased state within the church is to educate and equip Christians in the truth. With Scripture as their guide, believers can be equipped to identify the men qualified and called to lead God's church. In turn, biblically qualified men will be able to faithfully preach the Word, counsel believers, and disciple the next generation. To this end, Pastor Nelson's book will prove a valuable tool.

This book is a perfect resource for both pastors and laymen. Pastor Nelson has explained the biblical structure of church leadership and the qualifications for church leaders in a clear, simple, and practical manner. Recognizing that biblical counseling is central to the pastoral role, Larry has artfully blended counseling principles and priorities into the explanation and application of the biblical text.

You can find longer and more detailed books on this subject; you can find more thorough books on this subject; you can find more academic works on this subject; but you will not find a more practical work. This book is designed to provide a simple, clear, and straightforward description of biblical church eldership and the qualifications for those who would serve in that role.

I have known Larry and his wife, Marian, for 25 years. He is a friend, a mentor, and a dear brother. I am convinced that his work on the subject will serve to bless churches of every size as they seek to obey the will of the Good Shepherd. May the Lord use this book to conform His church to the biblical and God-glorifying structure He has established.

Jim Osman, Pastor
Kootenai Community Church
Kootenai, ID
November 2020

x

TABLE OF CONTENTS

Foreword	vii
Introduction	1
Chapter 1 Biblical Form of Church Government by Elders	3
Chapter 2 Biblical Qualifications for Church Elders	11
Personal Qualifications of Moral Character	19
Public Qualifications of Godly Reputation	49
Parental Qualifications of Family Leadership	62
Pastoral Qualifications of Sound Teaching	72
Chapter 3 Biblical Pattern for Recognizing and Installing Elders	93
Chapter 4 Biblical Counseling of Those Who Desire to Become Elders	97
Chapter 5 Biblical Treatment of Church Elders by the Congregation	105
Chapter 6 Biblical Counseling and the Process of Church Discipline	113
Chapter 7 Biblical Treatment of Disqualified Elders	119
Conclusion	123
Appendix – A Biblical Counseling Assignments to Assist in the Discipling of Elders and Those Who Would Seek to Become Elders	125
Appendix – B "To Drink or Not to Drink? — That is the Question"	139
Bibliography	151

INTRODUCTION

From Pentecost to the present, the church has been faced with constant and ever-widening problems concerning biblical theology and its practical applications to Christian living. Although these issues are of paramount importance to the spiritual health of God's people, in most cases they are not being biblically addressed because there is a leadership crisis in the church. Even among the minority of churches today which practice a New Testament form of church government by elders, there is nothing less than a famine of biblical understanding as to the high qualifications that these leaders must meet before they can be allowed to serve in this position. Consequently, men (and women) who are not biblically qualified are being placed into church leadership positions; and the results have been disastrous. Sadly, most pastors and laymen alike would find it difficult to recite even a dozen of the biblically-defined qualifications for church elders. Although some may choose to divide the pie differently, there are more than thirty biblical qualifications that must be clearly in place before anyone should be allowed to serve as a church elder. Even though these qualifications are biblically mandated as prerequisites to serving as an elder, it should become the personal goal of every Christian to carefully develop them, in the power of the Holy Spirit, as we cooperate with God in the sanctification process.

Most would agree that any given local church will not rise above the spiritual caliber of its leadership. And, when shepherds are not biblically qualified, both they and the sheep who follow them will most certainly go astray. Doctrinal error will inevitably lead to less than Christlike living. Therefore, Christians, as a whole, must become fully informed as to the biblical qualifications of those who are to lead Christ's church. As this takes place, it will become evident that many who are currently serving in leadership positions must either resign or be removed because they are not biblically qualified. This situation, and its surrounding ramifications, will result in a great need for biblical counseling to take place. Church leaders and members alike need clear guidance, help, and hope as they seek to navigate a new biblical course which brings honor and glory to God; and it is my prayer that the pages of this book will provide a clear and biblical path to follow.

The doulos of Christ,

Pastor Larry

*Whether, then, you eat or drink or whatever you do,
do all to the glory of God.
(1 Corinthians 10:31)*

CHAPTER 1

BIBLICAL FORM OF CHURCH GOVERNMENT BY ELDERS

Jesus said, "... I will build My church; and the gates of Hades will not overpower it" (Matt 16:18).[1] Every Christian, and especially church leaders, must constantly keep in mind that the church belongs to Christ and not to us. Therefore, its Founder and Owner has the right to establish how it functions best to the glory of God. Fortunately, none of this was left up to chance or the opinions of individuals through the centuries. As the Apostolic period of leadership was coming to an end, Paul made it abundantly clear that there was only one form of biblical church government, and that was to be leadership by biblically-qualified elders. Whether it was to the well-established and mature church of Ephesus pastored by Timothy, or to the newly established churches in Crete led by Titus, they were to be led and governed by elders. In Ephesus, the elders were already clearly in place leading the church, and Paul merely reminds Pastor Timothy of their necessary qualifications (1 Tim 3:1-7). However, Titus was instructed to "... set in order what remains and appoint elders in every city" of Crete (Titus 1:5). To set in order (epidiorthoo) means to make something straight, such as the setting of bones

---

[1] Unless otherwise indicated, biblical quotations are from the *New American Standard Bible* (La Habra: Lockman Foundation, 1995)

or the straightening of broken limbs. It is from this word that we get orthodontics and orthopedics.[2] The young church in Crete was apparently without proper leadership, and Titus was instructed to correct the problem.

Unfortunately, what God sets in order, man often seeks to alter for his own ends and to his undoing. Nowhere is this more true than within the church. Dr. Ladd, a professor at Fuller Theological Seminary, writes: "It appears likely that there was no normative pattern of church government in the apostolic age, and that the organizational structure of the church is no essential element in the theology of the church."[3] Quite the contrary, there is more clear and specific biblical instruction concerning church leadership than many of the other church issues, including the Lord's Supper, the Lord's Day, baptism, and spiritual gifts.[4]

Unbiblical thinking has caused the church to experiment with unbiblical and reactive forms of church polity. The episcopal form of church government was the result of elder shepherding leadership degenerating into power-driven echelons of ruling hierarchy. This perversion of God's order has been clearly exemplified in the Roman Catholic Church from about the fourth to the twenty-first centuries. Here, the Pope, cardinals, bishops, and church counsels make decisions for local parishes who are hundreds and even thousands of miles away.

Congregational church government formed as a reaction to the abuses of various episcopal denominations. After the

---

[2] John MacArthur, Jr, *MacArthur New Testament Commentary: Titus* (Chicago: Moody Press, 1996), 20.

[3] George Eldon Ladd, *A Theology of the New Testament*: (Grand Rapids: William B. Eerdmans Publishing Company, 1974), 534.

[4] Alexander Strauch, *Biblical Eldership: An Urgent Call to Restore Biblical Church Leadership* (Littleton: Lewis and Roth Publishers, 1995), 103.

Protestant Reformation of the sixteenth century, the proverbial pendulum began to swing to the opposite extreme, where all decisions rested with the individual members of any given local congregation. This also violates the biblical mandate of church government by godly elders. One need only observe in congregational church history how often God-honoring biblical programs are thwarted by an unrighteous minority. Some of these fine churches are thus prevented from moving forward. One large Conservative Baptist Church in the west grew from a Bible study of five couples to a church of over 1800 in just four years. They thought that they had an excellent Church constitution, which mandated a 90% vote of their membership before motions could be ratified. As this church finally came to realize, rather than being governed by the 90%, it was constantly being hamstrung by the 10%. This growing problem forced the pastor to go back to Scripture where he discovered his error, and through careful exposition of the Word, he instructed his congregation, which eventually embraced the biblically-mandated elder form of church government.

The Bible provides two, and only two, distinct offices in the church, elders *(presbuteros),* and deacons *(diakonos).* Simply put, the elders lead and make policy, and the deacons serve the elders, following their leadership and carrying out their directives. By way of biblical example, all of the following churches were governed by elders: the church at Jerusalem (Acts 15:2, 23); the church at Ephesus (Acts 20:17; 1 Tim 3:1-7; 5:17-25); the churches of Crete (Titus 1:5); the churches of Asia minor: Pontus, Galatia, Cappadocia, Asia, and Bithynia (1 Pet 1:1; 5:1); the church at Thessalonica (1 Thess 5:12-13); the church at Philippi (Phil 1:1); the churches of Derbe, Lystra, Iconium, and Antioch (Acts 11:30; 14:23); and the churches of the *diaspora* (Jas 5:14-15; Heb 13:17). No other form of church government was even hinted at. During the last five centuries, much has been done to both promote and cement biblical inerrancy into the hearts and minds of Bible-believing churches. And as a result, many Christians today are well-grounded in the fundamentals of the faith. However, for most of God's people, their understanding of God's design for biblical church government and the qualifications of those who would govern it is seriously deficient.

There are three Greek words in the New Testament which are all used to describe the same church leadership office: *presbuteros, episkopos,* and *poimen.* Depending on the English translation, they are rendered: *presbuteros* (elder/presbyter); *episkopos* (bishop, overseer, and guardian); and *poimen* (pastor and shepherd). *Presbuteros* (elder) speaks of a man's spiritual maturity. *Episkopos* (overseer) speaks of a man's authority and leadership skills. *Poimen (pastor)* speaks of a man's love for shepherding God's flock. Doctor Luke demonstrates the unity of these leadership descriptions in Acts 20:17, 28, where he uses *presbuteros, episkopos*, and the verb form of *poimen* to speak of and to the same men.[5]

The church must understand that there is no hierarchical structure intended by the use of these words; they are merely descriptions of the same office. The elders are not merely a church committee of directors who seek to carry on the business

---

[5] Acts 20:17; 28-31 – "From Miletus he sent to Ephesus and called to him the elders *(presbuteros)* of the church. ... 'Be on guard for yourselves and for all the flock, among which the Holy Spirit has made you overseers *(episkopos)*, to shepherd *(poimen)* the church of God which He purchased with His own blood. I know that after my departure savage wolves will come in among you, not sparing the flock; and from among your own selves men will arise, speaking perverse things, to draw away the disciples after them. Therefore be on the alert, remembering that night and day for a period of three years I did not cease to admonish each one with tears.'"

of the church in a businesslike manner. Elders are pastors. Passages such as Acts 20:17, 28-31[6] and James 5:14-15[7] should make it clear to all that the ministry of shepherding God's flock was not given to some higher echelon of church leadership called pastors. In every sense of the word, pastors are elders and elders are pastors. However, the unfortunate reality is that elders are most often seen as merely assistants to the pastor,[8] where he leads and all the others merely follow. "Yes men" have no place in church leadership. In such cases, there is only the appearance of a biblical leadership of peers, when in fact, the reality is that there is no one to check and balance the pastor(s).

Largely because of a lack of biblically-qualified elders, many churches today have sought to circumvent these biblical mandates by inventing unbiblical tiers of leadership where the pastor, who may be the only biblically-qualified elder in the church, does not even get a vote on the church governing board. In such cases, the biblically-defined office of the elder is often replaced by deacons; deacons are replaced by trustees, which is an office that has no biblical foundation, and the congregation must vote to approve matters of any significant (or in many cases insignificant) importance. Although this is certainly not always the case, trustees are often men who do not even biblically qualify to be deacons. Typically, they tend to be successful businessmen and/or administrators who have the authority to approve or disapprove most of the church's financial

---

[6] Idem.

[7] James 5:14-15 – "Is anyone among you sick? Then he must call for the elders of the church and they are to pray over him, anointing him with oil in the name of the Lord; and the prayer offered in faith will restore the one who is sick, and the Lord will raise him up, and if he has committed sins, they will be forgiven him."

[8] Strauch, op.cit., 15.

expenditures, which in a very real sense gives them the authority of elders without having to meet any of the biblical requirements. Instead of modeling after biblical mandates, this organizational structure looks more like corporate America. Paul's command in Romans 12:2, "And do not be conformed to this world ..." most certainly applies to churches, which seek to pattern their governmental structures after the world's mold rather than the mandates of Scripture. In churches which do not recognize the biblical office of elder, where deacons serve in this capacity, the serving position of deacon is replaced with trustees who often carry out the biblical role of deacon but without having to meet the biblical qualifications. Francis Schaeffer writes,

> The church has no right to diminish these standards for the officers of the Church, nor does it have any right to elevate any other as though they are then equal to these which are commanded by God Himself. These and only these stand as absolute.[9]

Sadly, other churches seek to create further unbiblical distinctions by not only separating pastors from elders, but they set up tiered echelons of authority among the pastoral leadership as well. The senior pastor is set apart with higher authority by naming other pastoral staff as associates or assistants to the pastor. Over the last five centuries, the protestant church has done much to separate itself from most of the extra-biblical false teachings and practices of Roman Catholicism; however, the terms senior and associate pastors often smack of the same unbiblical structures found among popes, cardinals, bishops, and priests. No such hierarchy exists among the biblical teachings on

---

[9] Francis A. Schaeffer, *The Church at the end of the 20th Century* (Downers Grove: InterVarsity Press, 1970), 65.

church leadership. Even Paul's admonition in 1 Timothy 5:17 to grant "double honor" to certain elders, "... especially to those who work hard at preaching and teaching," has nothing to do with authority or ranking within the eldership. Verse 18 explains that the "double honor" is speaking of their overall value to the church; namely, that such elders are to be well paid.[10] Any titles which may be used within the eldership should describe the focus of the man's ministry rather than some unbiblical pyramid structure.

Some biblically-qualified men who serve as elders are loathe to be called Pastor simply because they are not employed by the church, or they feel intimidated because of their lack of formal education. Others will accept the title Elder, but not Pastor because they know that they are not qualified. However, if a man is not biblically qualified to be a pastor, then he is also disqualified to serve as an elder because they are one and the same office. It does not matter if the elder is paid or unpaid, part-time or full-time in his service to Christ's church, he is to be a pastor in every sense of the word.

American democracy comes largely from a reaction to the British monarchy that abused its power rather than serving its subjects.[11] Wanting to have our hand in every piece of the decision-making pie is woven into the very fabric of American society. Therefore, it should be no surprise that over the last two hundred years, fear of abusive government has easily found its way into the church. Add to that at least sixteen hundred years of ecclesiastical abuses in Roman Catholicism, it should be no wonder that congregational government seems to be the

---

[10] 1 Timothy 5:18 – "For the Scripture says, 'You shall not muzzle the ox while he is threshing,' and 'The laborer is worthy of his wages.'"

[11] Strauch, op. cit., 39.

majority choice in North American churches today. But congregational church government, as it is commonly practiced today, is certainly not the answer. God's people should have no fear of biblically-qualified, loving leaders. English historian, Lord Acton (1834-1902), warned, "Power tends to corrupt, and absolute power corrupts absolutely."[12] However, a biblically-practiced eldership called to govern Christ's church provides for accountability that will set up hedges to rein in human depravity. The answer to our fears of abuse is not congregational control, but Holy Spirit control.

Let there be no doubt that God's call for a biblical eldership in His church will rock many North American churches to their very foundations. But in spite of whatever difficulties may arise in the elder form of church government, it is still biblical, and therefore non-negotiable. Jesus is the divine Architect of His church, and He alone has the authority to lay down the blueprint for both its government and the qualifications of its leaders.

---

[12] Ibid., 42.

CHAPTER 2

BIBLICAL QUALIFICATIONS FOR CHURCH ELDERS

Just as the Lord did not leave the form of church government open to the opinions of men, He also established exacting non-negotiable biblical standards by which prospective and current elders are to be scrutinized to determine their fitness for leadership. Christians must always remember that the church belongs to Christ. Therefore, He alone has the right to establish the qualifications of those who would lead it. These biblical standards are not mandated to punish men; rather, they are given to protect God's church from leadership that will inevitably bring moral and spiritual harm to His people and a reproach against Christ's name in the community. Simply put, some men are fit for elder leadership and some are not. Some men lack the spiritual maturity and gifting required of an elder. For others, personal sin, depending on its severity, can either temporarily or permanently disqualify a man. Although many churches today pass over these biblically-mandated disqualifications, we must neither lower the bar nor raise it higher than God does in His Word.

The gender qualifications for those who would serve as elders have nothing to do with geographical or cultural issues; neither are they affected by the passing of time. Although there is strong pressure among many churches today to ordain women as elders, this is clearly forbidden in Scripture. Not only does Paul always use male pronouns to describe elders, but he builds a theology which excludes women from leadership both in the home and in the church. Ephesians was, in part, written to address severe problems that Pastor Timothy was admonished to correct. One such problem was that women were apparently trying to usurp authority over their husbands and over other men in the church. In Ephesians 5:22-24,[1] wives are commanded to submit to their husbands. If God intended women to be elders in His church, then the rest of Paul's commands on this subject would have set up an untenable double standard of submission in the home and leadership in the church. Quite the contrary, he goes on to firmly correct this unbiblical behavior in 1 Timothy 2:11-12.[2] Simply put, women are forbidden to be placed into a position of teaching men in the church setting. First Corinthians was also an epistle written to correct serious problems in the church. In 14:34-35,[3] Paul brings a similar exhortation to women, where they are forbidden even to speak in the church service, unless they are clearly under the submissive leadership of their husbands (11:3-16).

---

[1] Ephesians 5:22-24 – "Wives, be subject to your own husbands, as to the Lord. For the husband is the head of the wife, as Christ also is the head of the church, He Himself being the Savior of the body. But as the church is subject to Christ, so also the wives ought to be to their husbands in everything."

[2] 1 Timothy 2:11-12 – "A woman must quietly receive instruction with entire submissiveness. But I do not allow a woman to teach or exercise authority over a man, but to remain quiet."

[3] 1 Corinthians 14:34-35 – "The women are to keep silent in the churches; for they are not permitted to speak, but are to subject themselves, just as the Law also says. If they desire to learn anything, let them ask their own husbands at home; for it is improper for a woman to speak in church."

Ephesians 4:11-12,[4] speaks of specially-gifted individuals who were called to equip the church for the work of service. The pastor *(poimen)* teacher *(didaskalos)* is not referring to two gifted individuals, but one, the pastor/teacher or teaching/shepherd.[5] Since all elders are to be involved in a teaching ministry[6] [7] and women are forbidden to teach men, then it should be clear to all that women are biblically excluded from being able to serve as church elders.

As we attempt to minister the Word of God to women, it is important for us to move the focus away from the prohibitions and onto the blessings of service which God has ordained for them. Titus 2:3-5[8] provides the framework upon which the woman, who wants to honor and glorify God, will build her life. She must lay aside any unbiblical aspirations to church leadership, in order to focus on godly character, behavior, and ministry to her husband, her children, and to the less mature women in the church. Rather than complain about that which she cannot have in the way of ministry, she should give thanks for

---

[4] Ephesians 4:11-12 – "And He gave some as apostles, and some as prophets, and some as evangelists, and some as pastors and teachers, for the equipping of the saints for the work of service, to the building up of the body of Christ;"

[5] MacArthur, op. cit., 21.

[6] 1 Timothy 3:2 – "An overseer, then, must be above reproach, the husband of one wife, temperate, prudent, respectable, hospitable, able to teach,"

[7] 2 Timothy 2:24 – "The Lord's bond-servant must not be quarrelsome, but be kind to all, able to teach, patient when wronged,"

[8] Titus 2:3-5 – "Older women likewise are to be reverent in their behavior, not malicious gossips nor enslaved to much wine, teaching what is good, so that they may encourage the young women to love their husbands, to love their children, to be sensible, pure, workers at home, kind, being subject to their own husbands, so that the word of God will not be dishonored."

that which God has ordained for her. In this, she will find her greatest joy, contentment, and fulfillment in life.

Once the gender issue has been settled, the Epistles go on to make it clear that qualifications for church elders fall into four basic categories: moral character, godly reputation, family leadership, and public ministry. Although there is certainly some overlap in the thirty-plus biblical qualifications for an elder, it is important to point out that most of these qualifications focus on who and what the man is in his walk with God, and from these, a man of proven godly character is deemed suitable or worthy to serve as an elder.

God has no double standards for His people. He does not have one list of moral character traits for elders and another for everyone else in the church. Church elders are, by the grace of God, to be the models of Holy Spirit-controlled godly character, as they minister to their families and to the church as a whole. Paul never said, "Don't do as I do; do as I say." Instead, he exhorted the church at Philippi to follow his example, saying, "The things you have learned and received and heard and seen in me, practice these things, and the God of peace will be with you" (Phil 4:9). He also exhorted pastors Timothy and Titus and entire churches to pave the way for others to follow.[9] It is

---

[9] 1 Timothy 4:12 – "Let no one look down on your youthfulness, but rather in speech, conduct, love, faith and purity, show yourself an example of those who believe."

Titus 2:7-8 – "In all things show yourself to be an example of good deeds, with purity in doctrine, dignified, sound in speech which is beyond reproach, so that the opponent will be put to shame, having nothing bad to say about us."

1 Corinthians 11:1 – "Be imitators of me, just as I also am of Christ."

Philippians 3:17 – "Brethren, join in following my example, and observe those who walk according to the pattern you have in us."

2 Thessalonians 3:7 – "For you yourselves know how you ought to follow our example, because we did not act in an undisciplined manner among you."

impossible to measure the wide-ranging impact and value to the church when godly Holy Spirit-controlled men are in leadership. But it is certainly not difficult to see the results of what happens when the opposite is the case. All the programs that the church can dream up, and all the money thrown at them, will never replace a biblically-qualified eldership. The following poem, by Joseph Malins (1895), illustrates the importance of proactive prevention rather than merely treating symptoms.

A Fence or an Ambulance
'Twas a dangerous cliff, as they freely confessed,
Though to walk near its crest was so pleasant;
But over its terrible edge there had slipped
A duke and full many a peasant.
So the people said something would have to be done,
But their projects did not at all tally;
Some said, "Put a fence 'round the edge of the cliff,"
Some, "An ambulance down in the valley."

But the cry for the ambulance carried the day,
For it spread through the neighboring city;
A fence may be useful or not, it is true,
But each heart became full of pity
For those who slipped over the dangerous cliff;
And the dwellers in highway and alley
Gave pounds and gave pence, not to put up a fence,
But an ambulance down in the valley.

"For the cliff is all right, if you're careful," they said,
"And, if folks even slip and are dropping,
It isn't the slipping that hurts them so much
As the shock down below when they're stopping."

So day after day, as these mishaps occurred,
Quick forth would those rescuers sally
To pick up the victims who fell off the cliff,
With their ambulance down in the valley.

Then an old sage remarked: "It's a marvel to me
That people give far more attention
To repairing results than to stopping the cause,
When they'd much better aim at prevention.
Let us stop at its source all this mischief," cried he,
"Come, neighbors and friends, let us rally;
If the cliff we will fence, we might almost dispense
With the ambulance down in the valley ..."[10]

When elders of godly character serve and lead by example as the fence at the top of the cliff, much of the ambulance work at the bottom of the cliff will be unnecessary. Jesus said, "... A blind man cannot guide a blind man, can he? Will they not both fall into a pit? A pupil is not above his teacher; but everyone, after he has been fully trained, will be like his teacher" (Luke 6:39-40). God's sheep will follow either the good or bad examples that are set before them in their leadership. In the days of Jeremiah, God testified against Israel's priests, prophets, and kings, who were ignoring God and His ways.[11] We hear God's lament in Jeremiah

---

[10] Joseph Malins, *The Best Loved Poems of the American People*, selected by Hazel Felleman (New York: Doubleday, 1936), 273.

[11] Jeremiah 2:8 – "The priests did not say, 'Where is the LORD?' and those who handle the law did not know Me; the rulers also transgressed against Me, and the prophets prophesied by Baal and walked after things that did not profit."

5:31,[12] where the people followed their leaders. Simply put, when leaders fail to measure up to God's moral standards, the bar is lowered for all who follow them. Individuals in the church will rarely rise above the moral character of their leaders. Many of today's pastors are guilty of the same sins practiced by Israel's leadership in Jeremiah's day. Instead of preaching the inerrant all-sufficiency of Scripture which provides "... us everything pertaining to life and godliness ..." (2 Pet 1:3), they preach a psychological, self-healing, good-feeling message that helps no one to know, or to honor, or to glorify, or to serve God.[13] One of the problems in the church at Ephesus was a corrupted leadership. Therefore, Paul exhorts Pastor Timothy in 1 Timothy 3:1-7 to remove the disqualified elders and to ordain righteous ones.[14]

There are no perfect churches or elders who serve them. When a biblically-qualified pastor comes into a new ministry, he often inherits the problems which the previous man either could

---

[12] Jeremiah 5:31 – "The prophets prophesy falsely, and the priests rule on their own authority; and My people love it so! But what will you do at the end of it?"

[13] Jeremiah 6:13-14 – "For from the least of them even to the greatest of them, everyone is greedy for gain, and from the prophet even to the priest everyone deals falsely. They have healed the brokenness of My people superficially, saying, 'Peace, peace,' but there is no peace."

[14] 1 Timothy 3:1-7 – "It is a trustworthy statement: if any man aspires to the office of overseer, it is a fine work he desires to do. An overseer, then, must be above reproach, the husband of one wife, temperate, prudent, respectable, hospitable, able to teach, not addicted to wine or pugnacious, but gentle, peaceable, free from the love of money. He must be one who manages his own household well, keeping his children under control with all dignity (but if a man does not know how to manage his own household, how will he take care of the church of God?), and not a new convert, so that he will not become conceited and fall into the condemnation incurred by the devil. And he must have a good reputation with those outside the church, so that he will not fall into reproach and the snare of the devil."

not, or would not, deal with. These problems can be compared to various sizes of holes in a boat, and the pastor must, of necessity, make two mental lists. The first list is entitled, "Holes (issues) that must be addressed immediately or the boat is going down." The second list is titled, "Holes that need to be plugged, but they can wait." And, it is wisdom from God's Word that will help him to understand the difference.

As the new pastor comes to lead, he comes with his experience and a measured amount of credibility with the church leadership and the congregation as a whole. This trust, which could be likened to credibility chips, will grow as he leads wisely. The more wise decisions he makes, the more chips he receives from those who are following his leadership. Regardless of the number and size of holes in any church boat, the pastor must work wisely to determine not only which ones need repairing, but when. Few if any new pastors have the chips to attempt making sweeping changes within the leadership or the congregation early on in their ministries. Often, he inherits congregational church government with no elders other than himself and deacons who are the governing board of the church. Sometimes, this board even has women serving on it alongside men.

As the pastor faithfully and wisely sets about to biblically instruct the church, in time, his pile of credibility chips will usually grow. This will not happen in weeks; it may even take years. But in God's time, and through patient teaching, the pastor can usually move the church and its leadership toward a biblically-based elder form of church government. Depending on how it takes shape, a congregationally governed church may eventually even vote itself out of a vote, as it installs biblically-qualified elders. During this time of teaching, some of the current deacon leaders will become mature elder-qualified men. Other deacons will move into more biblically defined areas of deacon service, while still others will resign from the board, realizing that they are biblically disqualified from deacon service. The point is that this all takes time and patience, and there is a name for the pastor who tries to accomplish all of this too soon, before he has enough chips. Actually, several come to mind: Foolish, Martyr, and Unemployed.

A. Personal Qualifications of Moral Character

As we consider the personal qualifications of biblically-qualified elders, it is essential to note at the outset that those who serve in this highest of all callings do so by the calling and the grace of God. Acts 20:28 says, "Be on guard for yourselves and for all the flock, among which the Holy Spirit has made you overseers, to shepherd the church of God which He purchased with His own blood." We must not only be on our guard concerning the enemies who will arise from both without and within the flock, but even more importantly, we must guard our hearts against pride, remembering that whatever we are, it is by the grace, and for the glory and honor, of God alone![15]

As one examines the biblical qualifications for church elders, it should be noted at the outset that the majority of them revolve around godly character. It is first the man's personal life that prepares him for service to others. Sadly, many churches today place far too much weight on a candidate's educational degrees, ministry experience, and eloquence in the pulpit, rather than on his godly moral character. Many churches are looking for pastors

---

[15] 1 Corinthians 15:9-10 – "For I am the least of the apostles, and not fit to be called an apostle, because I persecuted the church of God. But by the grace of God I am what I am, and His grace toward me did not prove vain; but I labored even more than all of them, yet not I, but the grace of God with me."

who are primarily good businessmen, administrators, managers, motivators, and even entertainers. However, these qualities only describe what a man does, not who he is. These externals may qualify a man for the business world, but they certainly do not qualify him to lead Christ's church. God's list of qualifications and disqualifications begins with a man's heart of moral character. When the Lord was preparing to reveal His choice for a king to replace Saul, no doubt Samuel was surprised when He rejected Jesse's handsome son, Eliab. In fact, He rejected seven older sons in favor of the youngest, David. We should all take a lesson from God's admonition to the prophet, "Do not look at his appearance or at the height of his stature, because I have rejected him; for God sees not as man sees, for man looks at the outward appearance, but the LORD looks at the heart" (1 Sam 16:7).

It is impossible to overestimate the power of example. There could be no greater joys in life than to know and to serve God. So there could be no higher calling than to lead men and women, boys and girls in these life-long pursuits. No one has a greater potential for good or for evil than pastors because sheep follow their shepherds. Richard Baxter exhorted all those who would serve as elders, saying, "Take heed to yourselves, lest your example contradict your doctrine ... lest you unsay with your lives what you say with your tongues; and be the greatest hinderers of the success of your own labors."[16] People are watching how we treat our wives and children and how we respond to those who disagree with us. Do we lead with gentleness and patience, or are we proud, harsh, and unkind?

A very pointed exhortation came from a fellow student in my first year Homiletics class to this young would-be pastor. "Be

---

[16] Richard Baxter, *The Reformed Pastor* (London: Banner of Truth, 1983), 61-63, 65.

careful what you teach because people will believe and follow you!" Jesus proclaimed this same truth in Luke 6:40, "... everyone, after he has been fully trained, will be like his teacher." In Hosea 4:9, the prophet laments one cause of the sinful condition of Israel, and he lays the blame at the feet of her spiritual leaders; "... like people, like priest ..." No one can measure the full extent of an elder's example either for good or for evil.

One obvious reason why God sets such high standards for those who would lead his church is because the individual Christians in the pew will rarely rise above the moral character of their pastoral leaders. When sin is tolerated in the leadership, it sets a new low in the comfort level for sin among the congregation.

1. Eagerness to Serve (1 Tim 1:1)

First Timothy 3:1 says, "... if any man aspires to the office of overseer, it is a fine work he desires to do." Two words in this text describe different aspects of his eagerness to serve. Aspire *(oregomai)* means to reach out for something, and desire *(epithumeo)* means to set one's heart upon something. He who would serve as an elder must be driven by a strong passionate compulsion to serve both God and His church. For the elder, regardless of whether or not he is paid by the church, shepherding God's church is not just one of many options he might pursue. Quite the contrary, this is his calling, his passion, his life's work. There are no other options! This "fine work" is hard work, which is often thankless and misunderstood by others. The shepherd is often tired and lonely, and yet, he is usually expected to be on call 24/7. And although he often tires in the work, he never tires of it. A man who does not have a passionate sense of God's calling on his life for this work will never be able to stay the course through all the vicissitudes of life and ministry.

2. One-Woman Man (1 Tim 3:2; Titus 1:6)

Both 1 Timothy 3:2 and Titus 1:6 say that the elder must be "...the husband of one wife..." Many opposing views have come forward seeking to explain the meaning of this phrase. First, we must understand what "... the husband of one wife..." is not. Some believe that Paul is prohibiting polygamy, which was never even addressed as a problem in the New Testament. Polygamy was illegal in the Roman empire during the First Century. It was rarely practiced because divorce was easy both among Romans and Jews alike.[17] One could conclude from 1 Corinthians 7:2 that it was also forbidden to all Christians when Paul exhorts, "But because of immoralities, each man is to have his own wife, and each woman is to have her own husband." Therefore, it would make no sense for him to make a special point of prohibition for church elders.

Some have asserted that "...the husband of one wife..." is prohibiting widowers, who have remarried, from being elders. Both 1 Timothy 5:14 and 1 Corinthians 7:39 encourage widows to remarry. It would be ludicrous to imagine that Paul would permit and encourage biblical remarriage for everyone but pastors![18]

---

[17] Mac Arthur, op. cit., 104.

[18] 1 Timothy 5:14 – "... I want younger widows to get married ... and give the enemy no occasion for reproach"

1 Corinthians 7:39 – "A wife is bound as long as her husband lives; but if her husband is dead, she is free to be married to whom she wishes, only in the Lord."

Others claim that "...the husband of one wife..." is prohibiting all divorced men from serving as elders. However, in Matthew 5:31-32 and 19:9, Jesus affirmed that divorce and remarriage were permitted in cases of adultery.[19] And Paul makes it clear in 1 Corinthians 7:15 that divorce was also permitted when it was initiated by an unbelieving spouse.[20] The point is that if the marriage vows are violated, the innocent spouse is not commanded to be held to the marriage bond. Even in the Old Testament, the immoral spouse was stoned to death, leaving the innocent spouse free to remarry and continue serving God. There is nothing here that would instantly prevent a man from serving as an elder just because he was divorced, whether it was before or after his conversion. However, if there are children of the dissolved marriage, they may very well disqualify him. It would be a very rare situation where an ungodly rebellious ex-wife would raise obedient Christ-honoring children. Although she is no longer part of the man's household, the children are, and as will be demonstrated later, rebellious children will most certainly disqualify a man from serving as an elder.

Another unbiblical interpretation of "... the husband of one wife ..." would prohibit single men from serving as elders. Paul encouraged, "... the unmarried and to widows that it is good for them if they remain even as I." (i.e., unmarried). Not only was

---

[19] Matthew 5:31-32 – "It was said, 'Whoever sends his wife away, let him give her a certificate of divorce;' but I say to you that everyone who divorces his wife, except for the reason of unchastity, makes her commit adultery; and whoever marries a divorced woman commits adultery."

Matthew 19:9 – "And I say to you, whoever divorces his wife, except for immorality, and marries another woman commits adultery."

[20] 1 Corinthians 7:15 – "Yet if the unbelieving one leaves, let him leave; the brother or the sister is not under bondage in such cases, but God has called us to peace."

Paul called an Apostle, but he also referred to himself as an elder.[21] Therefore, as a single elder, he most certainly was not prohibiting other single men from becoming elders.

The clear focus of the "... husband of one wife ..." qualification has nothing to do with a man's marital status; it is speaking directly to his moral condition. If he is married, then he must be a one-woman man. His eyes, his heart, and his desires are devoted to only one woman, his wife! However, there are some men who have remained married to the same woman for over fifty years, who are not one woman men. Consider men like Job, who said, "I have made a covenant with my eyes; how then could I gaze at a virgin? (Job 31:1). Jesus warned in Matthew 5:28, "... everyone who looks at a woman with lust for her has already committed adultery with her in his heart."

Nothing will mark a man's character for good or for evil more than his devotion to his wife, or the lack thereof. He who would serve Christ's church as an elder must be known for his moral purity. Many years ago, a very dear old widow said to me, "The main reason I voted for you to come and pastor our church was because of the way you treat your wife."

Although Paul was not married when he was writing his epistles, he never lost sight of the possibility that even he could fall. In 1 Corinthians 9:27, he gives this testimony concerning his personal discipline, in order to prevent his own disqualification from the ministry. "I discipline my body and make it my slave, so that, after I have preached to others, I myself will not be

---

[21] 1 Timothy 4:14 – "Do not neglect the spiritual gift within you, which was bestowed on you through prophetic utterance with the laying on of hands by the presbytery." *(i.e. elders)*

2 Timothy 1:6 – "For this reason I remind you to kindle afresh the gift of God which is in you through the laying on of my hands."

disqualified." No husband can be above reproach who is not a one-woman man! And no moral defect will disqualify him faster than the lack of it. The names Jim Baker and Jimmy Swaggart will always be remembered by this generation for the horrible reproach of moral impurity which blighted their lives and ministries. Strangely, few will remember or care about their numerous doctrinal aberrations and false teachings. History will only remember them as hypocritical immoral men who brought shame and disgrace upon the church and gave the enemies of Christ reason to blaspheme. Paul set the standard that he exhorted all Christians to follow, saying,

> "Whether, then, you eat or drink or whatever you do, do all to the glory of God. Give no offense either to Jews or to Greeks or to the church of God; just as I also please all men in all things, not seeking my own profit but the profit of the many, so that they may be saved" (1 Cor 10:31-33).

And again, he urged the Corinthian church to give "... no cause for offense in anything, so that the ministry will not be discredited" (2 Cor 6:3). Proverbs 6:32-33 says, "The one who commits adultery with a woman is lacking sense; he who would destroy himself does it. Wounds and disgrace he will find, and his reproach will not be blotted out."

3. Temperate (1 Tim 3:2)

To be temperate *(nephalios)* means to be wineless or unmixed with wine.[22] It means to be vigilant and clearheaded, one who is controlled by the Holy Spirit and the Word of God rather than by liquor or anything else. Ephesians 5:18 commands

---

[22] Mac Arthur, op. cit., 105.

and warns, "... do not get drunk with wine, for that is dissipation, but be filled with the Spirit." There are lessons to be learned both positively and negatively from the three highest callings in the Old Testament. Those who served as priests were forbidden to drink wine.[23] The Nazarite vow was the highest step of consecration that a person could make before God, and he, too, was forbidden to drink wine.[24] Kings were also warned about the dangers of having their judgment clouded by liquor.[25] In Isaiah 28:7, the prophet lamented over the horrible effects of drunkenness among those who were supposed to represent God in their day. "And these also reel with wine and stagger from strong drink: The priest and the prophet reel with strong drink, they are confused by wine, they stagger from strong drink; they reel while having visions, they totter when rendering judgment."

Church elders are neither priests, nor Nazirites, nor kings. They are far more, for they lead the church of God; and as such, they set the example for all who will follow them. They, above all, must be sound in judgment and clear-headed at all times, not be given to excesses in any area of life. Pastors must also be extremely careful where they lead their weaker brothers in Christ, lest by their example they cause others to stumble. Jesus knew how to be "... a friend of tax collectors and sinners" (Luke 7:34), and yet, He never participated in their sinful behaviors.

---

[23] Leviticus 10:9 – "Do not drink wine or strong drink, neither you nor your sons with you, when you come into the tent of meeting, so that you will not die--it is a perpetual statute throughout your generations."

[24] Numbers 6:2-3 – "... When a man or woman makes a special vow, the vow of a Nazirite, to dedicate himself to the LORD, he shall abstain from wine and strong drink ..."

[25] Proverbs 31:3-5 – "Do not give your strength to women, or your ways to that which destroys kings. It is not for kings, ... to drink wine, or for rulers to desire strong drink, for they will drink and forget what is decreed, and pervert the rights of all the afflicted."

Even so, in spite of His sinless life, He was misjudged for His associations.

Paul devoted Romans 14 and 1 Corinthians 8:1-13 to the Christian's responsibility to his weaker brethren in the faith. Although the subjects of these chapters are not alcohol, the principles learned here still apply. He was concerned about anyone who, by seeing his example of eating meat which had been sacrificed to idols, might become caught up in idol worship and the trappings connected to it. So, he chose to limit himself, not out of legalism but because of love for God and his weaker brethren. He concludes by exhorting, "Do not tear down the work of God for the sake of food ... It is good not to eat meat or to drink wine, or to do anything by which your brother stumbles" (Rom 14:20-21).

Apparently, Pastor Timothy had made a commitment to total abstinence when it came to wine, and that in a culture where the drinking of mixed wine (wine and water) was common and acceptable. Although we are not told the specific reasons for his abstinence, the aforementioned issues certainly could have influenced him. What we do know is that Paul knew this and instructed him, saying, "No longer drink water exclusively, but use a little wine for the sake of your stomach and your frequent ailments" (1 Tim 5:23). Drunkards often defend their debauchery by referencing Timothy's drinking of wine, but it should be noted that Paul had to exhort him to do so, and it was only for medicinal purposes.[26]

For a more complete study dealing with Christians drinking alcoholic beverages, go to APPENDIX – B "To Drink or Not to Drink? — That is the Question."

---

[26] John MacArthur, Jr, *MacArthur New Testament Commentary: 1 Timothy* (Chicago: Moody Press, 1995), 110.

4. Prudent / Sensible (1 Tim 3:2; Titus 1:8)

To be prudent or sensible *(sophron)*, means to be sound in mind, self-controlled, and moderate in opinion and passion. It is only used four times in the New Testament speaking of elders (1 Tim 3:2; Titus 1:8) and of mature godly women (Titus 2:2, 5). A prudent person is serious rather than frivolous, and he leads an ordered life. He is cautious in making decisions, and those decisions are made in accordance with the Word of God, not whims of the moment. Simply put, he thinks and acts biblically, as one who never disgraces either the gospel or his ministry by foolish behavior.

5. Free from the Love of Money: Contentment (1 Tim 3:3; Titus 1:7)

Both 1 Timothy 3:3 and Titus 1:7 speak of another character requirement for those who would serve as elders in Christ's church. Both use *aischrokerdes*, but they are translated differently. First Timothy says he must be "... free from the love of money," while Titus says he must not be "... fond of sordid gain." Clearly, just having money is not the problem. It is the love of money that pulls a man into obtaining it dishonestly, (i.e., sordid gain). Hebrews 13:5a speaks to the very heart of the matter saying, "Make sure that your character is free from the love of money, being content with what you have." The battle over greed versus contentment takes place in the inner man, where character is forged into the image of Christ. Paul warned Timothy again about the state of some men's hearts in the last days when they "... will be lovers of self, lovers of money *(philarguros)* ..." (2 Tim 3:2). *Philarguros* means to be a lover of silver. "For the love of money *(philarguros)* is a root of all sorts of evil, and some by longing for it have wandered away from the faith and pierced themselves with many griefs" (1 Tim 6:10). Paul set the example, saying that he did not lust for any man's silver or gold (Acts 20:33). The elder does not serve for the purpose of gaining money, power, and possessions,[27] but as a loving parent, he "... will most gladly spend and be expended ..." (2 Cor 12:14-15) for the glory of God and the good of others. Paul explained again why we are to serve, "For the love of Christ controls us ..." (2 Cor 5:14). God's leaders do not prostitute their calling by pursuing wealth. Instead, they must pursue holiness for the glory and honor of God and the good of others. He who would serve as an elder in Christ's church must "put off" the love of money and "put on" both contentment (Phil 4:11) and generosity as he remembers Jesus' admonition, "It is more blessed to give than to receive" (Acts 20:35).[28] Elders are called to shepherd God's flock, not to fleece it.[29]

---

[27] Philippians 4:11-13 – "Not that I speak from want, for I have learned to be content in whatever circumstances I am. I know how to get along with humble means, and I also know how to live in prosperity; in any and every circumstance I have learned the secret of being filled and going hungry, both of having abundance and suffering need. I can do all things through Him who strengthens me."

[28] It is noteworthy that this quotation of Jesus is not found in any of the gospel records. The simple explanation of this is that it falls under the purview of the last verse of the Gospel of John, where he asserts, "And there are also many other things which Jesus did, which if they were written in detail, I suppose that even the world itself would not contain the books that would be written" (John 21:25).

[29] 1 Peter 5:1-2 – "Therefore, I exhort the elders among you, as your fellow elder and witness of the sufferings of Christ, and a partaker also of the glory that is to be revealed, shepherd the flock of God among you, exercising oversight not under compulsion, but voluntarily, according to the will of God; and not for sordid gain, but with eagerness;"

6. Not Conceited / Proud or a New Convert (1 Tim 3:6)

The elder must not be a new convert (*neophutos*), which literally means one who is newly planted.[30] How often churches err by mistaking giftedness for maturity in the faith. The warning here is that immature believers will often become conceited (*tuphoo*), which literally means to be enveloped in smoke. They have their noses in the air, their heads in the clouds, and they do not know that they are heading for a fall. They are confused in the fog of their own self-deception; yet, others may see their pride clearly. If the devil, who was a perfect creation of God, could fall into pride, how much more does the church need to guard young converts from too much responsibility too soon. The violation of Paul's warning would find this young convert becoming conceited where he would then "... fall into the condemnation incurred by the devil" (1 Tim 3:6). Satan became proud, and God pronounced His judgment upon him, cutting him down from his high position. Paul here warns that when new converts are elevated too soon to leadership positions, the same thing will happen to them.[31] First Timothy 5:22 commands, "Do not lay hands upon anyone too hastily and thereby share responsibility for the sins of others..." Titus had been instructed by Paul, concerning the church in Crete, to "...set in order what remains and appoint elders in every city..." (Titus 1:5). The laying on of hands was the ceremonial setting apart of a man for pastoral or missionary service (Acts 13:2-3). Many a man and many a church has been ruined by the hasty appointing of a man

---

[30] George W. Knight III, *The Pastoral Epistles: A Commentary on the Greek Text* (Grand Rapids: William B. Eerdmans Publishing Company, 1992), 171.

[31] John MacArthur, Jr, *MacArthur New Testament Commentary: 1 Timothy* (Chicago: Moody Press, 1995), 117-118.

to a position of leadership before he is spiritually mature and scripturally trained for the rigors of pastoral service.

Maturity and stability take time to develop. Young believers are typically full of their own problems as God is pruning off large limbs of the old life. It is the young in the faith and immature whom Paul calls, "... children, tossed here and there by waves and carried about by every wind of doctrine, by the trickery of men, by craftiness in deceitful scheming" (Eph 4:14). To place a man in leadership too soon is tantamount to the blind leading the blind.[32]

Interestingly enough, Paul's instruction to Timothy, which prohibited new converts from being placed into leadership positions in Ephesus was not repeated to Titus for the churches in Crete. The Ephesian church would have had many mature and seasoned Christian men because Paul had taught there for two years at the school of Tyrannus. However, for the churches in Crete, just about everyone was a new convert when compared to Ephesus. So, elders need to be chosen from the most spiritually mature relative to the maturity of their congregations.[33]

It must be noted that sinful pride knows no age boundaries. Some men who have been Christians for years still have their heads enveloped in clouds of self-serving pride. Every believer, regardless of his age, will do well to remember Paul's questions to those who were proud in the Corinthian church. "For who regards you as superior? What do you have that you did not receive? And if you did receive it, why do you boast as if you had not received it?" (1 Cor 4:7). Whatever we have by the way of health, wealth, and/or position are gifts from God, and they must

---

[32] D. Martin Lloyd-Jones, *Preaching and Preachers* (Grand Rapids: Zondervan Publishing House, 1971), 109.

[33] Idem.

be received with gratitude and humility so that we can use these resources for His honor and glory and for the good of others.

Most certainly, there is no time when a Christian can say that He is free from the temptation to be proud. One woman stood up in a prayer meeting to give testimony saying that she had not sinned in word, thought, or deed in over thirty years. Clearly her words betrayed the sinful pride in her heart, and certainly, total depravity makes such a claim impossible, even in our best moments. Solomon had personal experience of his admonition, "Pride goes before destruction, and a haughty spirit before stumbling" (Prov 16:18). Paul's command to "flee idolatry" (1 Cor 10:14) comes after this solemn warning, "Therefore let him who thinks he stands take heed that he does not fall" (1 Cor 10:12). Every Christian, not just elders, must "put off" self-worshiping pride and "put on" Christlike humility every moment of the day.

7. Humble Servanthood (Matt 23:11-12)

Jesus taught that spiritual leadership must be marked by humility: "But the greatest among you shall be your servant. Whoever exalts himself shall be humbled; and whoever humbles himself shall be exalted" (Matt 23:11-12). And Paul warned all Christians, not just elders, "And do not be conformed to this world, but be transformed by the renewing of your mind, so that you may prove what the will of God is, that which is good and acceptable and perfect" (Rom 12:2). All would be well to note the contrast between Jesus and the religious leaders of His day. He was gentle and humble as opposed to His proud, arrogant, and selfish counterparts.[34]

---

[34] Matthew 11:28-30 – "Come to Me, all who are weary and heavy-laden, and I will give you rest. Take My yoke upon you and learn from Me, for I am

As Special Counsel to President Richard Nixon, Charles Colson experienced firsthand the corrupting nature of power and position on those who are not under the control of Christ.

> Nothing distinguishes the kingdoms of man from the kingdom of God more than their diametrically opposed views of the exercise of power. One seeks to control people; one seeks to serve people; one promotes self, the other prostrates self; one seeks prestige and position, the other lifts up the lowly and despised.[35]

> Power is like salt water; the more you drink the thirstier you get. The lure of power can separate the most resolute of Christians from the true nature of Christian leadership, which is service to others. It is difficult to stand on a pedestal and wash the feet of those below.[36]

In Mark 10:35-45, we see James and John seeking power rather than servanthood. Others became indignant, standing up for their personal rights. Sadly, many pastors today are driven by their craving for notoriety, praise, and an always bigger church. And many others in smaller ministries are jealous of those in larger ones. But success must never be determined by any of these outward vestiges. Moses was a huge success in the eyes of men when he struck the rock the second time around, but in the eyes of God, he was a horrible failure. And so severe was his failure that God forbade him from entering into the Promised Land. Success in the eyes of God is measured not in the results,

---

gentle and humble in heart, and you will find rest for your souls. For My yoke is easy and My burden is light."

[35] Charles Colson, *Kingdoms in Conflict,* (Grand Rapids: Zondervan, 1987), 274.

[36] Ibid., 272.

but in a man's humble faithfulness and obedience to God's commands. A pastor may be considered hugely successful in the eyes his congregation, but be an utter failure in God's sight.[37]

In the midst of Jesus' last words and instructions to His disciples concerning His coming death, Luke records, "And there arose also a dispute among them as to which one of them was regarded to be greatest" (Luke 22:24). Jesus' response to their unbelievable selfishness was,

> The kings of the Gentiles lord it over them; and those who have authority over them are called 'Benefactors.' But it is not this way with you, but the one who is the greatest among you must become like the youngest, and the leader like the servant. For who is greater, the one who reclines at the table or the one who serves? Is it not the one who reclines at the table? But I am among you as the one who serves (Luke 22:25-27).

John 13:1-17 picks up the story at this point and records Jesus' washing of His disciples' feet and His instruction to them.

> You call Me Teacher and Lord; and you are right, for so I am. If I then, the Lord and the Teacher, washed your feet, you also ought to wash one another's feet. For I gave you an example that you also should do as I did to you. Truly, truly, I say to you, a slave is not greater than his master, nor is one who is sent greater than the one who sent him. If you know these things, you are blessed if you do them (vv.13-17).

---

[37] Kent and Barbara Hughes, *Liberating Ministry from the Success Syndrome* (Wheaton: Tyndale House Publishers, Inc., 1987), 36.

Some churches today practice actual foot washing ceremonies; but they have clearly missed the entire point of what Jesus was trying to teach, for everyone comes with clean feet to offer a service to others, who have no need of it. However, Jesus donned the garments and duties of a common servant rather than that of a priest, setting an example of love and servanthood for all church leaders who would follow. Later He would bear the shameful cross and the sin of mankind as the suffering Servant. Today's elders must take a lesson in loving and humble servanthood from our Lord.[38] Paul's life and leadership also emulated humble servanthood. He said, "For we do not preach ourselves but Christ Jesus as Lord, and ourselves as your bond-servants (*doulos:* slave) for Jesus' sake" (2 Cor 4:5). And again Paul declared, "Let a man regard us in this manner, as servants (*huperetes*: under-oarsman galley slave) of Christ and stewards of the mysteries of God" (1 Cor 4:1).

Humility before God and men is a mandate that all Christians are called to obey. James 4:6,10 says, "But He gives a greater grace. Therefore it says, 'God is opposed to the proud, but gives grace to the humble' ... Humble yourselves in the presence of the Lord, and He will exalt you." As we seek, by the grace of God, to humble ourselves, God does not need to bring discipline and/or punishment into our lives to assist in the process. As elders, worldly authoritarianism must have no place in our lives and ministries. Whatever authority we have is God-given, and as

---

[38] Philippians 2:5-8 – "Have this attitude in yourselves which was also in Christ Jesus, who, although He existed in the form of God, did not regard equality with God a thing to be grasped, but emptied Himself, taking the form of a bond-servant, and being made in the likeness of men. Being found in appearance as a man, He humbled Himself by becoming obedient to the point of death, even death on a cross."

such, must be carefully and biblically implemented as the sacred trust of His servants.

8. Not Self-willed (Titus 1:7)

Titus 1:7 refers to the church elder as "God's steward" *(oikonomos)*. A steward was one who had responsibility and authority over another person's property or household. Joseph, in the Old Testament, was a faithful manager over Potiphar's entire household. Even so, the elder exercises his God-given role as a manager over God's property, the church. And like Joseph of old, elders must see their responsibility as a sacred trust. The church does not belong to them, but they have an awesome responsibility to lead, feed, and protect it. The verse continues in the same theme, by saying that the elder must not be self-willed *(authades)*, meaning he must not be arrogant or self-pleasing, asserting his personal will, with no regard as to how his words, attitudes, and actions will affect others.[39] Rather, he is to please God by serving His church as one "... who will give an account ..." (Heb 13:17) for the souls whom God entrusted into his care. Therefore, the elder must not be overbearing (NIV), meaning that he does not push to get his own way. First Peter 5:3 warns shepherds about "...lording it over those allotted to your charge..." The shepherd's role is that of leadership, not dictatorship.

The self-willed pastor has little, or no interest in truly listening to others' suggestions and/or criticisms. He comes across as one who always has to have his own way,[40] but he must

---

[39] John MacArthur, Jr, *MacArthur New Testament Commentary: Titus* (Chicago: Moody Press, 1996), 35.

[40] Warren Wiersbe, *Bible Exposition Commentary, Vol 2:* (Wheaton: Victor Books, 1989), 261.

remember that he is a pastor and not an abominable Pope. It is interesting to note the close association that Paul makes with self-willed elders and those who are quick-tempered (*orgilos*), which means soon angry. Self-willed people are really self-loving people who have a short fuse when they do not get their own way. They rule by fear and intimidation, and many are blind to their own sinful methods of leadership. If they cannot get their own way by convincing the rest of the elders as a group, they seek to divide and conquer. These sinful attitudes and actions must have no place in the godly elder's life.

John spoke of such a man, Diotrephes, who was the self-proclaimed church boss, a self-willed man, if ever there was one (3 John :9-10). John levels many accusations against him. First, he is described as one "... who loves to be first among them ..." Second, he "... does not accept what we say." Third, he is "... unjustly accusing us with wicked words ..." Fourth, "... he himself does not receive the brethren ..." And finally, he puts those who disagree with him "... out of the church." Sadly, there are many such men in church leadership positions today. Such men do not nurture, lead, and feed God's sheep; instead, they wound and scatter them for their own selfish ends. Simply put, these men must be removed from office, as John said he would do to Diotrephes upon his return, for they serve neither the church nor sinners when they insist on having their own way. Jesus instructed His disciples to be the antithesis of a self-willed person, saying,

> ... You know that the rulers of the Gentiles lord it over them, and their great men exercise authority over them. It is not this way among you, but whoever wishes to become great among you shall be your servant, and whoever wishes to be first among you shall be your slave;

just as the Son of Man did not come to be served, but to serve, and to give His life a ransom for many. (Matt 20:25-28)

Paul sought to live as one who constantly had the glory of God and the well-being of others at the forefront of his life. He gave exhortation and personal testimony to these Spirit-controlled goals in 1 Corinthians 10:31-33, "Whether, then, you eat or drink or whatever you do, do all to the glory of God. Give no offense either to Jews or to Greeks or to the church of God; just as I also please all men in all things, not seeking my own profit but the profit of the many, so that they may be saved."

9. Team Player (Acts 15)

Another essential requirement of a man who would serve Christ's church as an elder is that he must see himself as a part of a larger team of biblically-qualified men. In 1 Corinthians 12-14, Paul spends a great deal of time expounding on the fact that individual Christians make up the body of Christ. He is the Head, and we are the members of His body, the church. And just like every Christian in the local body needs all the others, so it is with the men who serve as elders. They all need one another because none of them individually have all the wisdom needed to lead Christ's church. As they share in the leadership ministry together, they will sharpen one another as "Iron sharpens iron ..." (Prov 27:17).

Nowhere in the New Testament do we find one elder lording it over another. Quite the contrary, they are always seen as a plurality of equals. In Acts 15, we have the record of how the young first-century church handled a serious doctrinal dispute that was upsetting the local church at Antioch. Eventually, Paul and Barnabas went up to Jerusalem to confer with the Apostles and elders in the hope of bringing a Christ-honoring resolution to the matter. Although there was debate, eventually they came to a unified conclusion, and they sent a letter detailing Christian doctrine and conduct. Note that there was no man-made pyramid structure in the early church, and the letter sent to the church at Antioch was the result of godly men both listening and deferring to one another as together they sought to determine the will of God in this particular situation. Robert Greenleaf addressed some of the dangers of abusive power, which were nowhere considered acceptable in the early church. He warned against the senior elder concept saying,

> To be a lone chief atop a pyramid is abnormal and corrupting. None of us are perfect by ourselves, and all of us need the help and correcting influence of close colleagues. When someone is moved atop a pyramid, that person no longer has colleagues, only subordinates. Even the frankest and bravest of subordinates do not talk with their boss in the same way as they talk with colleagues who are equals, and normal communication patterns become warped.[41]

So the question needs to be asked before a man is ever allowed to serve as an elder, "How well does he work and cooperate with others in the church?" One who is self-willed and arrogant in his dealings with others before becoming an elder will only get worse once he finds his way into this leadership position. And once he is there, it can be worse than pulling teeth trying to get him removed.

---

[41] Robert Greenleaf, *Servant Leadership: A Journey Into the Nature of Legitimate Power and Greatness* (New York: Paulist Press, 1977), 63.

10. Not Double-tongued (1 Tim 3:8)

Although this text speaks of the qualifications of deacons (*diakonos*)(men) and deaconesses (women), there is clear internal evidence that elders must also have these qualifications. Both verse eight and verse eleven begin with "likewise," which means in the same way. In this case it means, "Just as I spoke about elders, so now I am speaking about deacons." Although most of the qualifications for deacons are identical to that of elders, there are three additional qualifications mentioned here that would also of necessity apply to elders as well. Certainly, God does not hold a lesser moral standard for the leaders of the church, elders, than He does for the servants of the church, deacons. Verse eight says deacons (and elders) are not to be double-tongued (*dilogos*), meaning that they do not tell one story to one person and different stories to others, depending on what will most benefit themselves. Simply put, they do not lie; they always speak the truth to everyone.

11. Biblically-clear Conscience (1 Tim 3:9)

Note again in verse nine that deacons (and elders) must have a clear (*katharos*) conscience, namely a pure or clean conscience as opposed to a defiled one. As we have seen, the elder and deacon must be above reproach. One may wrongly say, "Well, I do not feel guilty, so I have a clear conscience." It is important here to remember that biblical guilt is not a matter of one's feelings; it is rather a state of being before a holy God. If we violate His Word, whether knowingly or unknowingly, we are guilty, and therefore, we need to repent. Paul speaks of those who are "by means of the hypocrisy of liars seared in their own conscience as with a branding iron" (1 Tim 4:2). But elders must follow the example of Paul, who said, "... I also do my best to maintain always a blameless conscience both before God and before men" (Acts 24:16). A clear or blameless conscience speaks well to the humility of the man, which is why it has been included in this section of personal character. A humble elder is eager to confess both to God and to men when he is wrong, and he is just as eager to seek their forgiveness. Godly elders keep short accounts with both God and men. Paul went on to affirm, "... the goal of our instruction is love from a pure heart and a good conscience and a sincere faith" (1 Tim 1:5). For those who would seek to instruct and/or lead others in the faith without a biblically-clear conscience are living in hypocrisy, mocking the Lord and His church, which they have been called to serve.

12. Not Malicious Gossips (1 Tim 3:11)

It should stand to reason that even though there are no specific prohibitions against gossip addressed to elders, Paul did make a special note of it in his instructions to deacons' wives. When one considers the high moral character that is required of elders, perhaps Paul considered this a given. However, since there are clear applications which can be derived for the elder, it will be included in the list.

First Timothy 3:11 teaches that the deacons' wives (and therefore elders) must not be "malicious gossips" (*diabolos*), which literally means devils, slanderers, or false accusers. A malicious gossip is one who shares negative and/or private information about another with someone who is neither part of the problem nor part of the solution. A man's spoken words reflect the integrity of his character in the inner man. Jesus made this clear in Luke 6:43-45. "For there is no good tree which produces bad fruit, nor on the other hand, a bad tree which produces good fruit ... The good man out of the good treasure of his heart brings forth what is good; and the evil man out of the evil treasure brings forth what is evil; for his mouth speaks from that which fills his heart." It is not enough to merely seek to control our words because words reflect the inner man.[42] When we deliberately seek the control of the Spirit of God in the inner man, our words will reflect "... love, joy, peace, patience, kindness, goodness, faithfulness, gentleness, and self-control ..." (Gal 5:22-23) rather than malicious gossip.

The counseling pastor must be especially careful with his speech outside his office. Although absolute confidentiality is unbiblical, (otherwise, the restorative church discipline spoken of in Matthew 18:15-17; 1 Corinthians 5; and Galatians 6:1-2; would never be possible), counselees must be assured that private conversations and disclosures will not be gossiped about. There is no faster way to kill a biblical counseling ministry than for pastors to be sharing private information with those who are neither part of the problem nor part of the solution. Even in counselor training classes, illustrative cases must be carefully chosen and shared in such a way as to not divulge confidences. It is best to keep to cases that are either long past or geographically separated from the local church setting. Even then, it is important to state these facts before any details of the case are shared. It is also essential to obtain permission from counselees to use their case information in class settings. This can be done initially through the Personal Data Inventory Counseling Application, or sometime during the actual counseling sessions. Even when such permissions are obtained, it is still a good idea

---

[42] Mark 7: 20-23 – "That which proceeds out of the man, that is what defiles the man. For from within, out of the heart of men, proceed the evil thoughts, fornications, thefts, murders, adulteries, deeds of coveting and wickedness, as well as deceit, sensuality, envy, slander, pride and foolishness. All these evil things proceed from within and defile the man."

to say something like, "I have been given permission to share this illustration from my counselee," before using it for illustration purposes. Otherwise, some in the congregation will not come for counseling, fearing that their case may become the next sermon or class illustration.

13. Loving What is Good (Titus 1:8)

The elder is to be known for "loving what is good" (*philagathos*), which means that he will love that which God loves. A good man will surround himself and his heart with other good men, books, music, and pastimes which give glory to God. Paul said in 1 Corinthians 10:31, "Whether, then, you eat or drink or whatever you do, do all to the glory of God." Godly elders will not subject their families or their churches to that which is not good in God's sight.

To be one who loves that which is good again speaks to the inner character of a man. Simply doing what is good and right is not enough. Two men could potentially do the same exact good things; however, for one God sees it as "gold, silver, precious stones," but for the other, it is "wood, hay, straw" to be burned up at the Judgment Seat of Christ.[43] The one thing which separates the two is motive. The why of biblical actions is everything. That which is done for the love of God and others both inside and outside the church has eternal value to our Lord

---

[43] 1 Corinthians 3:11-15 – "For no man can lay a foundation other than the one which is laid, which is Jesus Christ. Now if any man builds on the foundation with gold, silver, precious stones, wood, hay, straw, each man's work will become evident; for the day will show it because it is to be revealed with fire, and the fire itself will test the quality of each man's work. If any man's work which he has built on it remains, he will receive a reward. If any man's work is burned up, he will suffer loss; but he himself will be saved, yet so as through fire."

and will be rewarded accordingly. However, even when we do good things, but with wrong motives, these are destined to go up in a cloud of smoke.

Sadly, some do that which is good solely because of the fear of punishment (i.e., choosing not to litter for fear of being fined). However, we must love doing good because we love God, and because we love Him, we will seek to honor Him from the heart, not just out of duty. Jeremiah 17:9-10 says, "The heart is more deceitful than all else and is desperately sick; who can understand it? I, the LORD, search the heart, I test the mind ..." When the Bible speaks of the heart it is not merely referring to one's emotions; it is speaking of the entire inner man. So when Paul affirmed this trustworthy statement, "... if any man aspires to the office of overseer, it is a fine work he desires (*epithumeo*) to do" (1 Tim 3:1), the elder must serve with motives that honor God. And he must regularly examine these motives because even though this is a fine work, it is often a hard and wearisome work. Many who say that they are being "burned out" of the ministry are in fact those who have allowed once Christ-honoring motives of love and service to degenerate into the drudgery of wearisome duty. Paul warned, "Let us not lose heart in doing good, for in due time we will reap if we do not grow weary" (Gal 6:9), and "... brethren, do not grow weary of doing good" (2 Thess 3:13). Men who are called of God to serve as elders of Christ's church will often be weary in the work, but they will not be weary of it.

14. Devout (Titus 1:8)

The elder must also be devout (*hosios*) or holy in the inner man. Although there are several different Greek words that are translated into English as holy, the root meaning of this word is to be different.[44] Devout Christians are to be different from the world and its sinful ways. Second Corinthians 5:17 further describes this man, "Therefore if anyone is in Christ, he is a new creature; the old things passed away; behold, new things have come." He does not "... love the world nor the things in the world ..." (1 John 2:15).[45] In his heart, he does not give devoted love (*agapao*), to worldly endeavors, which only belongs to God and His people.

The devout man does not compartmentalize between Christian work and secular work. He is a Christian, and he is therefore in Christian work no matter what he does to make a living. We have all heard the foolish accusation, "He is so heavenly-minded, he is of no earthly good!" However, in point of fact, right living, which honors God and serves mankind, begins with right thinking; i.e., holy thinking about God and His Word. The devout man spends much time in the Word, in prayer, and in humble biblical self-examination. For him, prayer is not merely an event; it makes up the very fiber of his everyday life in all his dealings as he prays "... without ceasing" (1 Thess 5:17). His study, his family, and his ministries are constantly bathed in prayer that God will be honored and that Christ will be lifted up in his inner life and outer walk. Spurgeon exhorted his students to model Christ's prayers as seen in the gospels by praying long in private but short in public.[46]

---

[44] Wiersbe, op. cit., 262.

[45] 1 John 2:15-16 – "Do not love the world nor the things in the world. If anyone loves the world, the love of the Father is not in him. For all that is in the world, the lust of the flesh and the lust of the eyes and the boastful pride of life, is not from the Father, but is from the world."

[46] Charles H. Spurgeon, *Lectures to My Students*. (Grand Rapids: Zondervan Publishing House, 1954), 62.

15. Self-control / Self-discipline (Titus 1:8; 1 Cor 9:27)

Titus 1:8 describes the elder as one who must be self-controlled or self-disciplined (*egkrates*). Because much, if not most, of the pastor's day is spent in private away from the public eye, he should neither look for nor expect regulation from others. Not only must he be a self-starter, but he must love God, his family, and his church so much that he needs no one other than God to hold him in check. Although accountability is certainly a good thing, no amount of external accountability will keep him away from secret sin if he, in fact, wants to go down that road. Self-control is part of the ninefold fruit of the Spirit described in Galatians 5:22-23, "But the fruit of the Spirit is love, joy, peace, patience, kindness, goodness, faithfulness, gentleness, self-control ..." This Holy Spirit-empowered fruit begins with love and is saturated with self-control. Even Paul lived with the weighty fact that he could not slack off from exercising self-discipline without disastrous results both to himself and to those whom he served.[47] Clearly, Paul was not speaking of the potential loss of his salvation, but rather, he fully understood the gravity of an undisciplined life which would disqualify him from his privilege of leading Christ's church. His point was simply this: If an athlete needs to exercise personal discipline to have any hope of winning a temporal earthly prize, how much more does the elder need to do so to remain in God's service. Because of our depravity, we can never eradicate the idols of our own heart, but by God's

---

[47] 1 Corinthians 9:25-27 – "Everyone who competes in the games exercises self-control in all things. They then do it to receive a perishable wreath, but we an imperishable. Therefore I run in such a way, as not without aim; I box in such a way, as not beating the air; but I discipline my body and make it my slave, so that, after I have preached to others, I myself will not be disqualified."

grace, we can and must mortify them.⁴⁸ The self-controlled man knows where he is tempted to worship that which is other than God, and he seeks the constant control of the Holy Spirit rather than feeding the lusts of his flesh. This battle is fought and won moment-by-moment by the grace of God in the inner man, as we seek to "put off" self-worship and "put on" thinking and living to the glory and honor of God.⁴⁹

16. Pleases God Rather Than Men (Galatians 1:10; 1 Thessalonians 2:3-4)

Proverbs 29:25 warns, "The fear of man brings a snare, but he who trusts in the LORD will be exalted." No doubt the fear of man is one of the most common disqualifiers of men in and from pastoral ministry. And sadly, many continue for years seeking the

---

⁴⁸ Romans 8:13 – "for if you are living according to the flesh, you must die; but if by the Spirit you are putting to death the deeds of the body, you will live."

⁴⁹ Ephesians 5:15-21 – "Therefore be careful how you walk, not as unwise men but as wise, making the most of your time, because the days are evil. So then do not be foolish, but understand what the will of the Lord is. And do not get drunk with wine, for that is dissipation, but be filled with the Spirit, speaking to one another in psalms and hymns and spiritual songs, singing and making melody with your heart to the Lord; always giving thanks for all things in the name of our Lord Jesus Christ to God, even the Father; and be subject to one another in the fear of Christ."

Ephesians 4:17-24 – "So this I say, and affirm together with the Lord, that you walk no longer just as the Gentiles also walk, in the futility of their mind, being darkened in their understanding, excluded from the life of God because of the ignorance that is in them, because of the hardness of their heart; and they, having become callous, have given themselves over to sensuality for the practice of every kind of impurity with greediness. But you did not learn Christ in this way, if indeed you have heard Him and have been taught in Him, just as truth is in Jesus, that, in reference to your former manner of life, you lay aside the old self, which is being corrupted in accordance with the lusts of deceit, and that you be renewed in the spirit of your mind, and put on the new self, which in the likeness of God has been created in righteousness and holiness of the truth."

praise of men rather than the praise of Almighty God. In the opening verses of his Epistle to the Galatians, Paul criticized some of them for turning away from the truth to a false gospel. Certainly, this rebuke was difficult for Paul to deliver and painful for this church to receive, but he immediately explains his motives for delivering it. "For am I now seeking the favor of men, or of God? Or am I striving to please men? If I were still trying to please men, I would not be a bond-servant (*doulos* – slave) of Christ" (Gal 1:10). Prior to his salvation, he did seek to please men, his rabbinical peers, by persecuting the church, all the while believing that he was pleasing God.[50] But once he was converted on the Damascus Road, all that was over. Clearly, he chose to "put off" whatever remained of the fear of man, and he "put on" his commitment to seeking to please God alone, regardless of what anyone else might think of him or do to him. Paul reiterated this same conviction to the Thessalonians.[51]

The courage of conviction for the glory of God and the good of His people must be central to all the words and works of church leaders. Elders must not only know God's Word, but they must be lovingly fearless in teaching it. This is not a license for unkindness or bullying, for Paul exhorted that Christians are to be known for "... speaking the truth in love ..." (Eph 4:15) lest our message be likened to a "... noisy gong or a clanging cymbal" (1 Cor 13:1). This courage of conviction is nothing less than a passion, which must proceed from the inner man of shepherds

---

[50] John MacArthur, Jr, *MacArthur New Testament Commentary: Galatians* (Chicago: Moody Press, 1987), 22.

[51] 1 Thessalonians 2:3-6 – "For our exhortation does not come from error or impurity or by way of deceit; but just as we have been approved by God ... so we speak, not as pleasing men, but God who examines our hearts. For we never came with flattering speech, as you know, nor with a pretext for greed-- God is witness-- nor did we seek glory from men ..."

who truly love God and His sheep, lest they become confused, scattered, and destroyed by the ravages of false teaching. Only a right and righteous fear of God will preclude the fear of man and the resultant misuse or trimming of the Word for one's personal gain and protection. Self-love and protection must be "put off" and replaced with God's sacrificial love and truth regardless of the personal cost.

B. Public Qualifications of Godly Reputation

The twofold truth of 1 Samuel 16:7 concerning the choice of David as the new king of Israel certainly applies to the biblical qualifications and disqualifications of the elders who would lead Christ's church. As has been previously discussed, God said to Samuel, "... man looks at the outward appearance, but the LORD looks at the heart." Personal qualifications of moral character are hidden in the heart of a man, and from this root comes the fruit of public behavior, which makes for a godly reputation. Jesus warned his disciples saying, "... every good tree bears good fruit, but the bad tree bears bad fruit. A good tree cannot produce bad fruit, nor can a bad tree produce good fruit" (Matt 7:17-18). Nowhere is this more true than in the life of a pastor, and time will reveal his inner moral character (or the lack of it) by his words and works. When it comes to a man's inner life, we can only ask him questions and pray that his answers are truthful, but eventually, his life will reveal his heart.

1. Above Reproach (1 Tim 3:2; Titus 1:6)

Anepileptos (1 Tim 3:2) and *anegkletos* (Titus 1:6) are both translated as above reproach. *Anepileptos* speaks primarily of a man's past, meaning that he cannot be held; namely, that there is no basis for arresting him on criminal charges. It speaks very much to his outward behavior in which there is no factual basis for blame or accusation. On the other hand, *anegkletos* is a present participle indicating his current manner of life. Certainly, he is not a sinless man. However, his life should not be so marred by sin so as to cause him to be disqualified.[52] There is to be no obvious defect which would lead others into sin, thus discrediting God and His work. Namely, there is no lasting residual disqualifying accusation or guilt that could render him unfit for service.

Even Peter was rebuked by Paul for his momentary hypocrisy in Galatians 2:11-21. Obviously, Peter repented of his sin and continued in his leadership service to the church. Because of Paul's pre-Christian past, where he persecuted the church, he referred to himself as the foremost of all sinners;[53] and yet, in Christ, he called us all to "... be blameless and innocent, children of God above reproach in the midst of a crooked and perverse generation, among whom you appear as lights in the world" (Phil 2:15). Again in 2 Timothy 2:19, Paul exhorts, "... Everyone who names the name of the Lord is to abstain from wickedness," and he goes on to describe such a one in verse twenty-one as being, "... a vessel for honor, sanctified, useful to the Master, prepared for every good work." This is to be our ongoing, life-long endeavor. First Timothy 6:14 says, "... keep the commandment without stain or reproach until the appearing of our Lord Jesus Christ." The phrase "above reproach" sets the descriptive

---

[52] John MacArthur, Jr, *MacArthur New Testament Commentary: 1 Timothy* (Chicago: Moody Press, 1995), 103.

[53] 1 Timothy 1:15 – "It is a trustworthy statement, deserving full acceptance, that Christ Jesus came into the world to save sinners, among whom I am foremost of all."

standard under which all the other subsequent moral qualifications will line up.

On one New Year's Day, a man called to say, "I've been watching your life for the last three years, looking for hypocrisy or any reason to reject what you teach, and I want you to be the first one to know that I have finally received Christ as my Lord and Savior." Truly, salvation is of God, but He uses godly examples to lead the way to Christ. Dr. John MacArthur, Jr. is reputed to have said, "It is not enough for a gardener to love flowers; he must also hate weeds. Even as doctors would not consider operating with dirty hands, neither should pastors preach and teach with a dirty life." Paul's exhortation in 2 Corinthians 6:3 applies to all Christians, but especially to pastors, "... giving no cause for offense in anything, so that the ministry will not be discredited." Although King David was not a pastor, the principle of Nathan's rebuke rings true as a warning for every pastor to be a man of godly character, both in public and in private. When David's adultery and murder were finally exposed, Nathan revealed this tragic result to his repentant king, "... by this deed you have given occasion to the enemies of the LORD to blaspheme ..." (2 Sam 12:14). If pastors are to be "above reproach," they must live as though they will never have any secrets, no skeletons in the closet that could one day bring shame to Christ and His church.

As has been previously discussed, the character of a one-woman man is found in the inner man, and that inner godliness will show in the way he behaves in the presence of other women and in the way he treats his wife, both in public and in private. Pastors must be living examples of this quality, men who, "... put on the Lord Jesus Christ, and make no provision for the flesh in regard to its lusts" (Rom 13:14). There is no more important area of his life where he must be above reproach, because unfortunately, a man need not be guilty to be put out of the ministry forever. He must only be accused and undefendable (his word against hers).

Back in 1948, Billy Graham and his evangelistic team covenanted together to live by the standard of 1 Thessalonians 5:22, "Abstain from all appearance of evil" (KJV). The practical outworking of this for Graham meant that, he would not travel, meet, or eat alone with a woman other than his wife. Over the years, this commitment has become known as "The Billy Graham Rule." However, changes of law and technology have brought new challenges into the 21st Century; and so many of us have seen the need to expand "The Billy Graham Rule," to say, "I will not under any circumstances travel, meet, eat with, counsel, or engage over media platforms such as Skype and FaceTime with any woman or minor child without my wife, or another adult witness being present."

Several years ago, my wife and I were called upon to minister to a woman who had a very young daughter who had been molested by her father. Once the fact that she had been sexually molested had been affirmed by other government-appointed professionals, the matter finally came before the court, where I was called upon to testify for the better part of three days. The father's attorney planned to blame the child's perverted behaviors on me, her pastor and counselor. However, because I had the reputation of practicing "The Billy Graham Rule" faithfully, and without exception, for over 30 years, this twisted false accusation never gained any traction.

The question may arise, "Is a pastor sinning who does not set up these safeguards?" Clearly, the Bible does not mandate them, so he has not sinned. However, Romans 13:14 does command us to "... make no provision for the flesh in regard to its lusts." So by implementing such safeguards, he will not only hedge in his own temptable flesh, but also he is protecting others from temptation. And having done everything in his power to protect his and God's good name, he prays for protection against temptation and false accusation.

2. Respectable (1 Tim 3:2)

The elder must be respectable (*kosmios*), meaning that he is known for his good and proper behavior. Again, it must be noted that outward behavior comes from within the heart of a man. He must be known as one who leads an orderly life rather than a life of chaos so that what he does on a personal, smaller, and less complicated level, he will reproduce in the church.[54] Jesus taught this principle in Luke 16:10: "He who is faithful in a very little thing is faithful also in much; and he who is unrighteous in a very little thing is unrighteous also in much." This is a man who knows how to stay on task until the job is done. However, he is careful not to make an idol out of orderliness and/or duty, but instead, he practices them for the glory of God and the good of His church.

He must be one who is known for the respectful ways in which he treats his wife and children both in public and in private. His God-honoring respectfulness must also extend from the home into the church and beyond into the world, and even to those who disagree with him. Dr. Walter Martin was known worldwide as an expert on cults for most of fifty years. Although he spoke with biblical clarity exposing the errors of false religions, he set an example of gracious respectfulness toward all who disagreed with him. He was a Christian statesman, who was known for "... speaking the truth in love ..." (Eph 4:15); and we would all do well to follow his example.

---

[54]MacArthur, op. cit., 107.

3. Hospitable (1 Tim 3:2; Titus 1:8)

One of the many things that clearly separates the leaders of Christ's church and men of worldly success is that the elder must be hospitable (*philoxenos*), meaning that he enjoys having guests in his home; literally, loving the stranger. In the world, the more successful or famous the man, the more he desires to live in privacy. He uses his wealth to shut people out of his life, while church elders are to be lovers of strangers. He seeks to open his home to those in need, all the while guarding his primary responsibility, that of caring for and protecting his own family. Some of the greatest lessons he will ever teach will not come from behind the pulpit, but rather from the laid-back atmosphere of his living room as he visits, encourages, and counsels, sometimes into the wee hours of the morning. Such times and places of warm fellowship let people experience their pastor interacting with his wife and family where they can see the reality of his life and the ways in which his wife and children respond to his leadership. It is not possible to shepherd effectively from afar. The pastor must be available to people, exercising hospitality from a willing and thankful heart as one who has received much from the hand of God and is therefore eager to share with the not-so-lovely of this world. One young teenage girl expressed unbridled excitement, as she and her parents were driving to our home for fellowship and a meal, saying, "We are going to get to see our pastor in his natural habitat!"

It is important to note again that these qualifications, as set forth for elders, should also be aspirations for the entire church. Peter exhorted all who are Christians to, "... keep fervent in your love for one another ... Be hospitable (*philoxenos*) to one another without complaint" (1 Pet 4:8-9). The writer of Hebrews reminds us all, "Do not neglect to show hospitality to strangers, for by this some have entertained angels without knowing it" (Heb 13:2). And when we prepare to have others into our homes, we should remember Jesus' admonition to share with those who cannot return our hospitality.[55] James identified a very important aspect of pure and undefiled religion as visiting "... orphans and widows in their distress ..." (Jas 1:27). Every time the word visit (*episkeptomai*) is used in the New Testament, it carries the sense of looking out for others in order to do them good, whether it be for the soul or the body, or both.

4. Not Quick Tempered (Titus 1:7); Not Pugnacious (1 Tim 3:3; Titus 1:7)

Quick-tempered (*orgilos*) men have no place in church leadership because their lack of self-control clearly evidences that they are not under the Holy Spirit's control.[56] The King James Version translates *me orgilos* as "not soon angry." *Orgilos* is derived from *orge*, which speaks of an internalized anger, the slow burn of a settled indignation. In time, *orge* will likely morph into *thumos*, a volcanic anger, which erupts to the damage and defilement of many. Such behaviors evidence idolatrous pride and a deep-seated bitterness, both of which will disqualify a man from pastoral service. An *orgilos* man is one who is known to

---

[55] Luke 14:12-14 – "... When you give a luncheon or a dinner, do not invite your friends or your brothers or your relatives or rich neighbors, otherwise they may also invite you in return and that will be your repayment. But when you give a reception, invite the poor, the crippled, the lame, the blind, and you will be blessed, since they do not have the means to repay you; for you will be repaid at the resurrection of the righteous."

[56] Galatians 5:22-23 – "But the fruit of the Spirit is love, joy, peace, patience, kindness, goodness, faithfulness, gentleness, self-control; against such things there is no law."

have a propensity to anger. He is short-fused and easily provoked.[57]

Quick-tempered (*orgilos*) anger will often escalate into further pugnacious (*plektes*) sinful behavior. A pugnacious man is one who is given to contention, quarreling, argumentation, fighting, and even the striking of others. He assaults others with words or even blows. Sadly, some pastors are able to mask their fleshly outbursts in public, while they reserve their worst behaviors for their families. Men of such two-faced hypocrisy have no place in the leadership of Christ's church.

James exhorts all Christians, not only elders, saying, "... everyone must be quick to hear, slow to speak and slow to anger; for the anger of man does not achieve the righteousness of God" (Jas 1:19-20). Paul instructed Pastor Timothy, "The Lord's bond-servant (*doulos* – slave) must not be quarrelsome, but be kind to all ... patient when wronged" (2 Tim 2:24). Bullies simply have no place in church leadership, or as Warren Wiersbe says, "Short tempers do not make for long ministries."[58] Proverbs 22:24-25 warns, "Do not associate with a man given to anger; or go with a hot-tempered man, or you will learn his ways and find a snare for yourself." Ephesians 4:30-32 exhorts Christians to "put away ... all bitterness and wrath and anger and clamor and slander ... along with all malice," because these sinful behaviors grieve the Holy Spirit. He then commands us to "put on" being, "... kind to one another, tender-hearted, forgiving each other, just as God in Christ also has forgiven you." The pridefully bitter man worships

---

[57] John MacArthur, Jr, *MacArthur New Testament Commentary: Titus* (Chicago: Moody Press, 1996), 36.

[58] Wiersbe, op. cit., 221.

at the altar of self-love, and as he fails to receive God's sanctifying grace, he regularly contaminates and defiles others.[59]

Serving as elders in Christ's church requires Holy Spirit-empowered self-control because elders are often misunderstood and maligned. But elders must set the example as those who, "Never pay back evil for evil to anyone ..." (Rom 12:17). They make every effort to "... be at peace with all men" (Rom 12:18) as they endeavor not to be "... overcome by evil, but overcome evil with good" (Rom 12:21).[60]

5. Gentle and Peaceable (1 Tim 3:3)

In stark contrast to being pugnacious, elders must be gentle (*epiekes*), meaning mild, moderate, and patient when listening to others. They are to be considerate and gracious, eager to pardon and work with others.[61] Christians are to be known as those who walk "with all humility and gentleness, with patience, showing tolerance for one another in love, being diligent to preserve the unity of the Spirit in the bond of peace" (Eph 4:2-3). Christians do not manufacture unity and peace within the body of Christ; we merely endeavor to preserve or to destroy them. The gentle man is eager to "put off" self-worshiping pugnaciousness, which destroys, and then "put on" Christ-honoring gentleness, which preserves the blood-bought unity of Christ in His church.

First Timothy 3:3 links being gentle with that of being peaceable (*amachos*). Elders are to be peacemakers, not

---

[59] Hebrews 12:15-16 – "See to it that no one comes short of the grace of God; that no root of bitterness springing up causes trouble, and by it many be defiled; that there be no immoral or godless person like Esau, who sold his own birthright for a single meal."

[60] MacArthur, op. cit., 39.

[61] John MacArthur, Jr, *MacArthur New Testament Commentary: 1 Timothy* (Chicago: Moody Press, 1995), 111.

troublemakers. Paul makes it clear that these attributes of being gentle and peaceable are not just required for elders in that he exhorts all Christians, "... to be ready for every good deed, to malign no one, to be peaceable, gentle, showing every consideration for all men" (Titus 3:1-2).

However, this is especially important for elders because their unity, or lack of it, will impact everyone in the church either positively or negatively. When the elders have their meetings, they above all others should be known for the gentle and peaceable Christlike manner in which they treat one another. Even when disagreements occur, they must do so agreeably as they seek the mind of Christ.

6. Good Reputation Outside the Church (1 Tim 3:7)

First Timothy 3:7 requires that the elder must "have a good reputation (*kalos marturia*) with those outside the church." Certainly, this does not mean that all the unbelievers in his community must like him, because when we become a friend and child of God, we pick up a lot of His enemies. Stephen was a godly man, and yet those outside the church hated him, and were so enraged by his testimony that they stoned him to death (Acts 7:54-60).[62] It is interesting to note that Stephen had an impeccable reputation (*marturia*), and it is from this word that the English word "martyr" is derived.[63] To have a good reputation means that the elder is not a hypocrite. Sadly, many unsaved

---

[62] Acts 7:54-60 – "Now when they heard this, they were cut to the quick, and they began gnashing their teeth at him ... But they cried out with a loud voice, and covered their ears and rushed at him with one impulse. When they had driven him out of the city, they began stoning him; and the witnesses laid aside their robes at the feet of a young man named Saul. They went on stoning Stephen as he called on the Lord and said, 'Lord Jesus, receive my spirit!' ..."

[63] MacArthur, op. cit., 119.

businessmen hate dealing with pastors because so many of them either do not pay their bills or they expect special discounts because they are in the ministry. Many pastors are bivocational in order to support themselves in the ministry, but some of these are lazy and/or even dishonest in their jobs working for unbelievers. These kinds of disgraceful behaviors disqualify a man from the ministry of being an elder, and they give both Christ and the church where they serve a bad name in the community. Paul, like Christ, blistered the religious leaders of his day for their hypocrisy, saying, "You who boast in the Law, through your breaking the Law, do you dishonor God? For the name of God is blasphemed among the Gentiles because of you ..." (Rom 2:23-24).

There will usually be some in the pastor's community who do not like him, but their accusations should never come as a result of unchristlike defects in his character. There were some in King Nebuchadnezzar's kingdom who were jealous of Daniel's position in the king's court. Oh, that all Christians would have such a testimony among their enemies, where the only legitimate accusation could be in regard to their selfless devotion to God and others.[64]

Church elders must be known in their communities for their strong moral character, love, kindness, generosity, goodness, and family leadership; even though there will always be those

---

[64]Daniel 6:4-5 – "Then the commissioners and satraps began trying to find a ground of accusation against Daniel in regard to government affairs; but they could find no ground of accusation or evidence of corruption, inasmuch as he was faithful, and no negligence or corruption was to be found in him. Then these men said, 'We will not find any ground of accusation against this Daniel unless we find it against him with regard to the law of his God.'"

who disagree with their theology.[65] Paul exhorts all Christians, not just elders, to "... prove yourselves to be blameless and innocent, children of God above reproach in the midst of a crooked and perverse generation, among whom you appear as lights in the world" (Phil 2:15). And Peter echos this same principle in 1 Peter 2:12, "Keep your behavior excellent among the Gentiles, so that in the thing in which they slander you as evildoers, they may because of your good deeds, as they observe them, glorify God in the day of visitation."

Elders must remember that they are not called to clean up the dead unregenerate corpses of the world. Many a well-intentioned pastor has needlessly damaged his reputation in his community by taking sides in the world's politics and/or other issues, which are not his to fight. Perhaps Paul had these potentially distracting and derailing issues in mind when he warned, "No soldier in active service entangles himself in the affairs of everyday life, so that he may please the one who enlisted him as a soldier" (2 Tim 2:4). It is one thing for him to preach and teach concerning the sin of abortion and euthanasia, but it is another thing entirely for him to picket or block the doors to abortion clinics. There are plenty of others, even other Christian laymen, who, if necessary, can participate in lawful community issues. However, pastors are called to reach the lost and to disciple the Church. These are full-time endeavors which require all his ministry focus. Therefore, he dare not siphon away his time on other issues which are, at best, distractions, and at worst, bear traps.

---

[65]John MacArthur, Jr, *MacArthur New Testament Commentary: Titus* (Chicago: Moody Press, 1996), 119.

7. Just (Titus 1:8)

In this context, just (*dikaios*) most likely means that elders are to be fair, wise, upright, righteous and equitable.[66] The pastor must be a man of unbending and unstained integrity. David describes this kind of man as one who, "... swears to his own hurt and does not change" (Ps 15:4). We would say, "He practices what he preaches," and "His word is his bond." He is not only upright, but he is equitable and fair to all, without partiality, never making decisions based upon personal favoritism. Paul rebuked the church at Corinth for taking their disputes into the secular courts rather than seeking to handle matters within the church. He asked, "... Is it so, that there is not among you one wise man who will be able to decide between his brethren ...?" (1 Cor 6:5). Clearly this was to be the duty and privilege of the church elders. But they were being sinfully bypassed in favor of the secular system.

The Bible speaks of God as being just (*dikaios*), when Jesus prayed, "O righteous (*dikaios*) Father ..." (John 17:25). Note the promise of 1 John 1:9, where again, (*dikaios*) is used to describe God's character, "If we confess our sins, He is faithful and righteous (*dikaios*) to forgive us our sins and to cleanse us from all unrighteousness." As Christians, we are all called to be just and righteous in all our doings, following our Lord as the example. Church elders must be wise biblical counselors, who are able to rightly and righteously lead Christ's church in the practical issues of everyday life to the glory of God and the good of His people.

---

[66]MacArthur, op. cit., 41.

C. Parental Qualifications of Family Leadership

Much can and should be learned about a man's potential abilities to lead the church as an elder by the way he parents and leads his family in general. Although Scripture never requires perfection of husbands and fathers, it does mandate a growing faithfulness of all who would serve as elders in Christ's church. Paul draws this matter into a sharp, and for some, an uncomfortable focus by asking what should be a common sense rhetorical question, "But if a man does not know how to manage his own household, how will he take care of the church of God?" (1 Tim 3:5). Simply put, poor management in the home will translate to worse management in the church, but Christ-honoring management in the home will extend to the same in the church. In the home, the man must only manage his own family and finances. However, in the church, he may need to care for hundreds of families with a correspondingly huge budget. Ergo, faithfulness in the smaller will translate to faithfulness in the larger. Unfortunately, many churches today simply ignore a pastoral candidate's home life, seeing it as mostly irrelevant to the job at hand. Some seem to believe that one has little or nothing to do with the other; while others, make a sort of unspoken pact with their fellow leaders, saying, "I won't ask about your family, if you won't ask about mine." Pastors can exhort their congregations about many things, but often they do not possess the personal credentials and courage to give biblical admonitions about what a Christ-honoring family is supposed to look like. However, Paul did not leave this extremely important matter unaddressed.

1. Manages His Own Household Well (1 Tim 3:4)

The elder's qualifications to serve Christ's church are not only those of personal character and public integrity, but they also reach into his home. Paul asserts that, "He must be one who manages (*proistemi*) his own household well" (1 Tim 3:4). Later in 5:17, he makes a clear connection between leadership and authority both in the home and in the church, where he speaks of "elders who rule (*proistemi*) well ..." Certainly, as *proistemi* is being used here, it carries no negative connotations of the arbitrary or harsh treatment that was commonly experienced under the ruling monarchs of his day. Christ's elders are not to be tyrants, either in the home or in the church. Instead, they are to rule well (*kalos*) or excellently. Paul makes an interesting choice of words here. He did not use (*agathos*), meaning morally or practically good. Instead he uses (*kalos*), meaning aesthetically good or appealing to the eye.[67] It is a given that the elder's home would of necessity be morally good, but this is not enough; it must also set an example and appeal to those who observe it. Whether a man is managing his home or Christ's church, he must keep in mind that he is merely a steward of that which God has placed into his hands. Neither the family nor the church belongs to him; and as God's steward, he does whatever is necessary for the good of both.

2. Keeps His Children Under Control with All Dignity (1 Tim 3:4)

Although this verse does not necessitate either marriage or children as a prerequisite for being an elder, if he is married with

---

[67] John MacArthur, Jr, *MacArthur New Testament Commentary: 1 Timothy* (Chicago: Moody Press, 1995), 116.

children, then they must be under control (*hupotage*). This is a military term meaning to line up in ranks under the one in authority, and they are to do so with all dignity (*semnotes*), meaning with respectful, well-disciplined, courteous, and humble behavior.[68] Rebellion or stubbornness in the ranks is not even an option.

There is nothing in this text that would imply that these children are sharing their father's faith in Christ, but even unsaved children must be controlled and required to obey. The elder must be known for "... keeping his children under control with all dignity (*semnos*)." Dignity is not referring to the pastor's children; rather it is referring to the manner by which their father keeps them under control. He leads in an honorable or venerable way, as opposed to yelling, threatening, and over-correcting. Ephesians 6:4 commands, "Fathers, do not provoke your children to anger, but bring them up in the discipline and instruction of the Lord."

A wise and godly father leads by authority, wisdom, and love. By his authority, he establishes rules which his children are required to obey, regardless of whether or not they are believers, and he is not afraid to bring age-appropriate consequences for disobedience, negligence, or disrespectful behavior. By wisdom, his rules are not arbitrary, and whenever possible, he explains the practical and moral reasons behind them in order to make obedience attractive. By love, and because of love both for God and for his children, the father teaches them to obey for the love of God and the joy of honoring Him through their obedience, as opposed to obeying only out of the fear of punishment.

---

[68] MacArthur, op. cit., 116-117.

Sadly, there are many pastors who are good preachers but bad parents. Such men must either learn how to biblically lead and control their families, or they need to get out of the pastoral ministry. He may be an outstanding man who practices personal godliness, but if his children are known for being foolish and out of control, he must then relinquish his position, at least for a time, until he is able to bring his family up to this minimal biblical standard.

3. Faithful Children (Titus 1:6)

Among all of the thirty-plus prequalifications for pastoral service, Paul's admonition "... *having children who believe (pistos)*, not accused of dissipation or rebellion," has caused some of the greatest disagreements and consternation among Bible scholars. The interpretation of the passage all seems to hinge on Paul's use and meaning of *pistos.* On one side of the issue, there are those who are absolutely convinced that *pistos* means "believing" or "saved" teenage and/or adult children. The other side is just as convinced that *pistos* is being used in its most general sense of being "faithful," (i.e., children being "faithful" to their parents). Unfortunately, neither side has presented an ironclad exegesis for its view, and both sides present what seem to be some unanswerable questions for the other. The point is that there are good men, outstanding theologians, on both sides of this issue. And as such, there needs to be honor and respect one for the other. No one will argue that the husband/father must be the spiritual leader in his home, and both sides agree on the 1 Timothy 3:4-5 requirement that an elder's children (even those who are still unbelievers) must be under the control of the father. In point of fact, each man and church must grapple with these issues and eventually determine how they will implement *pistos* in the elder-qualifying process.

For those who advocate *pistos* to mean "believing children," they cite that Paul uses *teknon*, the most general term to describe one's offspring regardless of age. Paul uses it in reference to "Titus, my true child (*teknon*) in a common faith ..." (Titus 1:4). They say that if Paul was wanting to use *pistos* as relating to young children, who were faithful to their parents, there are Greek renderings he could have used other than *teknon* to indicate their age. Believing children advocates maintain that since Paul uses *teknon,* he must be referring to children of any believing age, which would include adult children.

Some "faithful children" advocates, who are for the most part excellent exegetes, make a very weak argument, saying that this places an unfair burden upon the father, who becomes personally responsible for the salvation of all his children if he is to enter and remain in the pastoral ministry. After all, salvation is of God, and no man can will his children into genuine salvation.[69] However, fairness to the father or somehow penalizing him for his unbelieving children is certainly not at issue here. For those who believe that salvation is solely the work of our sovereign God, and that He therefore elects those of His choosing for salvation, the objection should be a moot point. For if God can and does elect a man to salvation and He wants that man to be in ministry, and if believing children were a requirement for that ministry, then God could and certainly would elect the man's children to be saved prior to any point of disqualification.

Some "believing children" advocates accuse the other side of a simple failure to exegete the Titus 1:6 as they would any other

---

[69] Strauch, op. cit., 229.

text. They maintain that a pre-exegetical bias prevents the "faithful children" advocates from honestly exegeting the text. Namely, if the text were honestly exegeted and embraced, then thousands of pastors and elders would be instantly out of the ministry. So they maintain that consequences rather than clear exegesis is driving the "faithful children" view. It is not uncommon to hear a "believing children" advocate ask of the other side, "What would the text mean if you had believing children?" This smug accusation couched in a question is not only cruel, but it is forbidden. Paul made it clear that only God is able to accurately "... disclose the motives of men's hearts ..." (1 Cor 4:5). So to make the aforementioned assumptions clearly reveals the critic's own arrogance and pride, which are in themselves disqualifications to pastoral ministry. If a man's children are believers, he should humbly rejoice in God's sovereign love and kindness. But to rub another man's nose in the fact that any or all of his children are not saved is simply cruel and can serve no Christ-honoring purpose.

Many "believing children" advocates often seek to support their view by linking Titus 1:6 to 1 Timothy 3:5, "But if a man does not know how to manage his own household, how will he take care of the church of God?" Their argument is that if his own children will not follow him in his faith, then why should anyone else? However, by linking these two texts in this way, they miss the whole point of the 1 Timothy passage. As has been previously proven, this text makes no mention of faith of the pastor's children. It is only requiring that they be under control.

If Paul was seeking to affirm that elders must have believing children, then he certainly could have used verbiage to communicate this more clearly and precisely. For example, there could be no question as to who was being addressed when he wrote 1 Corinthians. "Paul ... To the church of God which is at

Corinth, to those who have been sanctified in Christ Jesus, saints by calling, with all who in every place call on the name of our Lord Jesus Christ, their Lord and ours." When it came time to write Titus 1:6, Paul could have easily used *en Christos* (i.e., *in Christ*) rather than *pistos*, and that would have been the end of it; no discussion and no speculation.

The 1 Timothy 3 and Titus 1 verses in question are clearly parallel passages, and there is nothing unclear or ambiguous about Paul's meaning in 1 Timothy 3:4 "He must be one who manages his own household well, keeping his children under control with all dignity." The issue here is controlled children, not saved children. Then in Titus 1:6, he says, "... having children who believe, not accused of dissipation or rebellion." Here again, the issue is control, not salvation. However, some proponents of the believing children view, when noting the sins of dissipation (*asotia*) and rebellion (*anupotaktos*), say that dissipation refers to participating in drunken pagan festivals, and rebellion refers primarily to political or military insurrection. In the family context, rebellious children would refuse to submit to parents and/or government.[70] They go on to affirm that the gravity of these sins could only be committed by older (i.e., adult) children. In such cases, fathers would still be disqualified from elder service even though these adult children would likely be living on their own, outside the parents' home and influence. But if Paul is affirming control rather than salvation in both of these parallel passages, then dissipation and rebellion would fit perfectly into the text. It takes no stretch of the imagination to think that teenage children, could still be living in the home, and become involved in such sinful activities. But the text does not affirm that

---

[70] John MacArthur, Jr, *MacArthur New Testament Commentary: Titus* (Chicago: Moody Press, 1996), 31.

they are actually doing these sinful things. It describes these children as not being "... accused of dissipation or rebellion." Clearly, Paul is exhorting the father to guard and guide his children, even in their associations. Namely, if you associate with those who practice dissipation and rebellion, you will be accused of it even if you are not guilty. Paul's point is that if a man cannot keep either his believing or unbelieving children under control and away from bad associations, then he cannot lead Christ's church as an elder.

Some proponents of the "believing children" view strongly affirm that every time *pistos* is used in the New Testament, it is always used of people who are believers; and even if the Titus 1:6 were accurately translated "faithful children" (i.e., faithful to their parents), they were only faithful because they were believers.[71] However, of the sixty-two verses in the New Testament where *pistos* is used, many of them do not specifically use it to describe believers. For example, in Jesus' Parable of the Talents (Matthew 25:14-30), He spoke of two men who were called faithful (*pistos*) slaves. Although Jesus compared them to faithful believers in His interpretation of the parable, they were just slaves in the story, who were faithful (*pistos*) to their master. The point is that even unbelieving slaves can be faithful to their master, but when Christians are faithful to their Lord, they receive eternal rewards.

It is important to note the destinations of these epistles to Timothy and Titus. Timothy was the pastor of the church at Ephesus, the place where Paul had taught and discipled "... daily in the school of Tyrannus ...for two years ..." (Acts 19:9-10). If ever there was a well taught and mature church in Asia Minor,

---

[71]MacArthur, op. cit., 30.

the Ephesian church was it. Titus, on the other hand, was left by Paul in Crete so that he, "... would set in order what remains and appoint elders in every city as I directed you" (Titus 1:5). To set in order (*epidiorthoo*) means to straighten that which is crooked or to set broken bones.[72] Clearly, there were some major problems that needed to be set straight in Crete. To the Ephesian church, which was mature and well-established, Paul instructs Timothy that he must not appoint new converts to the position of elder. However, no such instruction is included for the churches of Crete. It stands to reason that all or most of the converts in Crete were relatively new in comparison to those in Ephesus.[73]

Another evidence that the churches of Crete were not peopled with the mature elder stock of Ephesus is that the elders of the churches of Crete were not required to "... have a good reputation with those outside the church ..." as were the elders of Ephesus. Quite possibly, the Christians of Crete had not been saved long enough to have undone bad reputations from the old life.

As one compares the mature church at Ephesus to the young churches on Crete, it would seem logical that there would be a greater percentage of men with believing children in the place where Paul had ministered for so long. And yet for the Ephesian church, he only requires elders to have their children under control. But if we are to accept the believing children view, we also have to accept that Paul had a double and unreasonable standard for the churches in Crete, who were much less likely to have a pool of potential elders, each with no unbelieving children.

---

[72] Ibid., 20.

[73] Knight, op. cit., 156.

It is interesting to note that neither the 1 Timothy 3 nor the Titus 1 passages say anything requiring the elder's wife to be a believer. It would seem ludicrous for Paul to require the man's children to be saved, and yet say nothing in these contexts about requiring him to have a believing wife. That is not to say that the elder could effectively serve with an unbelieving wife. In fact, when Paul wrote to the Corinthians, he asked the question, "Do we not have a right to take along a believing wife, even as the rest of the apostles and the brothers of the Lord and Cephas?" (1 Cor 9:5). So the point remains, it would make no sense for Paul to speak in 1 Timothy and Titus of the necessity for believing children and not also speak clearly about requiring a believing wife.

Even though those who hold to the "believing children" view of Titus 1:6 are clearly in the minority, there are still many good men who have been barred from elder service, even though they are otherwise biblically-qualified. It is one thing to exclude a man who has unruly children, but it is quite another to bar him from elder service without biblical cause. Many men have been faithful fathers, keeping their children under control all their growing up years, only to have some of these same children leave home as unbelievers. Parents who live with the heartache of unsaved adult children need to be counseled biblically to have right theology concerning who is ultimately responsible for salvation. Although it is the parents who are responsible to teach God's Word and to live consistent Christ-honoring lives before their children, it is ultimately God alone who brings them to salvation. Fathers need to embrace their biblical responsibilities and to trust in God's good and sovereign choices when it comes to the salvation of their children.

Sadly, some men who are biblically disqualified because of their unruly children still try to strong-arm their way into church leadership. In such cases, as with all biblical disqualifications, these men need to be counseled to humbly embrace their circumstances with a renewed zeal to reach out to their children, who must become the main focus of their ministry. A man with unruly children simply does not have time for ministry outside the home. But as he focuses upon developing faithful children, he someday will likely be mature enough to focus some of his ministry time outside the home. Like it or not, the home is the proving ground for determining a man's ability to lead the church, and although it is a hard truth, some men are simply not qualified. When churches allow them to serve in elder positions of leadership, they not only dishonor God by violating His Word, but they also do great harm to the church as a whole by lowering the standard for everyone. Christian individuals will rarely rise above their leaders, and that is why God sets the bar so high for those who would serve as church elders.

D. Pastoral Qualifications of Sound Teaching

Almost all of the previously-stated biblical qualifications for elders are repeated by Paul regarding those who would serve as deacons. While deacons by definition are called to be servants along with the elders, there is a clear biblical distinction between them. God significantly raises the qualification bar in that elders must be very skillful in biblical teaching. Paul instructed Titus in his choosing of elders that they had to be known for:

> ... holding fast the faithful word which is in accordance with the teaching, so that he will be able both to exhort in sound doctrine and to refute those who contradict. For there are many rebellious men, empty talkers and deceivers, especially those of the circumcision, who must be silenced because they are upsetting whole families,

teaching things they should not teach for the sake of sordid gain. (Titus 1:9-11)

1. Holds Tenaciously to the Word of God (Titus 1:9)

The elder must be active in "... holding fast (*antechomai*) the faithful word ..." of God. "Holding fast" literally means "to hold one's self to," namely, "to adhere to." Elders are to be glued to the Word of God. When it comes to exegeting the Bible and leading of the church, his personal opinions have no place. Second Peter 1:20 says, "But know this first of all, that no prophecy of Scripture is a matter of one's own interpretation." Elders must not look for personal interpretations and leading in the white space. Paul exhorted Pastor Timothy, "Be diligent to present yourself approved to God as a workman who does not need to be ashamed, accurately handling the word of truth" (2 Tim 2:15). Accurately handling (*orthotomeo*) literally means to "cut it straight." In other words, "Make it your goal to study hard, so as to make all the pieces fit." Learning to cut it straight is a lifelong endeavor which usually takes years of study and being taught before one can faithfully lead and feed God's church. Many so-called pastors are starving God's sheep because of their ineptness in studying and communicating God's Word. It is no wonder that Paul exhorts in 1 Timothy 5:22, "Do not lay hands upon anyone too hastily and thereby share responsibility for the sins of others ..."

Since the early 1900s, the church has continued to fight well in the battle for biblical inerrancy. However, we hear very little today from Bible-believing seminaries about biblical sufficiency. Notice how the Apostle Peter affirmed this magnificent hope-filled truth. "Grace and peace be multiplied to you in the knowledge of God and of Jesus our Lord; seeing that His divine power has granted to us everything pertaining to life and godliness, through the true knowledge of Him who called us by His own glory and excellence" (2 Pet 1:2-3). It is not enough to affirm the inerrancy of Scripture without being committed to the sufficiency of Scripture. Peter's affirmation makes it clear that by God's Word and through the power of the indwelling Holy Spirit, Christians have everything they need for life and godliness (i.e., salvation and sanctification). Everything is a superlative, meaning that there is nothing more that is needed. All issues of the Christian's life have biblical answers, which the elder must learn, live, and be prepared to share.

2. Able to Teach (1 Tim 3:2) and Exhort in Sound Doctrine (Titus 1:9)

There is a clear and logical progression in the Titus 1:9-11 passage. Once the elder has a good grasp of God's Word, he then has the responsibility to exhort in sound doctrine. However, no one can give that which he does not have, and nowhere is this more true than when it comes to biblical knowledge and practical exposition. First Timothy 5:17 speaks of elders "... who work hard at preaching and teaching." This is not sweating in the pulpit; it is laboring hard in the preparation. When Paul says that the elder must be able to teach (*didaktikos*), he means that he must be a skilled teacher who is "... constantly nourished on the words of the faith and of the sound doctrine ..." (1 Tim 4:6).[74]

It is also important to note that the teaching qualification mandates for elders in both Titus 1 and 1 Timothy 3 are set in the context of moral character and personal living. His deeds and doctrines, his practice and precepts, his life and lip must never be

---

[74] John MacArthur, Jr, *MacArthur New Testament Commentary: 1 Timothy* (Chicago: Moody Press, 1995), 108.

separated. Even excellent teachers can be disqualified by a dirty life. When a pastor questioned a disgruntled member of his church as to the reason for his leaving, he replied, "What you are speaks so loudly, that I cannot hear what you are saying!" Just as we cannot give what we do not have, we must never seek to teach what we do not know. It takes years of study to become competent in the Scriptures, which is another reason why young believers are not to be teachers. After years of study, we say that doctors are still practicing. While medical malpractice can result in death, pastoral malpractice is far worse. Sadly, church history is replete with incompetent pastors who misled entire congregations.

However, the Bible nowhere mandates that God's shepherds must be trained by formal schools of biblical instruction. Speaking of Jesus in John 7:15, "The Jews then were astonished, saying, 'How has this man become learned, having never been educated?'" And again, the same was said by them about Peter and John, "Now as they observed the confidence of Peter and John and understood that they were uneducated and untrained men, they were amazed, and began to recognize them as having been with Jesus" (Acts 4:13). Paul was the only one of the disciples who had formal rabbinical training, and much of that had to be jettisoned and replaced with truth. That said, no one should despise formal biblical training in that it can certainly speed up the process of preparing for a lifetime of elder ministry. However, such graduates, even from the best schools, must realize that knowledge is not tantamount to wisdom.

Many men today have spent their entire educational lives moving from one Christian school to another, and that without being involved in any significant Christian ministries. In the process, they may have gained an excellent grasp of theology, but many of them have little or no life experience, no pegs upon which to hang their learning. Such men will do well to not jump into a solo pastorate, although they may be tempted to do so, thinking that their years of learning will see them through. There is much more to pastoring than the preparation and delivery of sermons. Without life experience, his sermons will be little more than the regurgitation of commentaries and the parsing of Greek verbs. He must be able to explain the text to others, with practical application, in such a way that it will challenge and change their lives. Young men in the ministry will do well to spend time being discipled by a seasoned pastor, who can give life and meaning to all their learning. John MacArthur has said, "Teaching sets the nails into the mind, but example is the hammer that drives them in deep."[75] In time, he will develop excellent communication skills, and like Paul, he will be able to say, "... knowing the fear of the Lord, we persuade men ..." (2 Cor 5:11). Godly pastors do not yell at their congregations from behind the pulpit. Rather, they seek to persuade them through the clear and practical exposition of the Word, a winsome life, and a kind and humble manner of speaking.

Study should lead to personal application and godly character, which in turn should lead to the effective exhortation (*parakaleo*) of others. Jesus promised in John 16:7 to send the Helper or Comforter (*parakletos*), meaning the Holy Spirit. These Greek renderings are merely the verb and noun forms of the same word. They both have the sense of "coming alongside to aid." So the elder who is trained in the Word can, by the power of the indwelling Holy Spirit, come alongside God's church to aid and encourage them in the truth. In a similar way but using different words, Paul exhorts the entire church at Rome saying,

---

[75] MacArthur, op. cit., 114.

"... my brethren, I myself also am convinced that you yourselves are full of goodness, filled with all knowledge and able also to admonish (*noutheteo*) one another" (Rom 15:14). Biblical knowledge coupled with Christian character are the credentials which must be in place before we can effectively exhort anyone.

No word of man can truly feed the souls of men, no matter how eloquent or inspiring it may be. Shepherds, who do not study the Word, will certainly starve God's sheep. Much preaching today is filled with emotion and little else. Emotion can be compared to water; it may be refreshing, but it contains no nourishment. Anyone who tried to live on water alone would starve to death. Many churches today are filled with emaciated sheep who are fed a steady diet of emotional man-centered preaching, believing it to be the Word of God; and they wonder why their life in Christ never grows? Dr. Martin Lloyd-Jones warned, "We have somehow got hold of the idea that error is only that which is outrageously wrong; and we do not seem to understand that the most dangerous person of all is the one who does not emphasize the right things."[76] Paul instructed the Ephesian elders to follow his example, saying, "... I did not shrink from declaring to you the whole purpose of God" (Acts 20:27). True shepherding pastors burn the midnight oil preparing healthy meals to the glory of God and the healthful growth of their flocks.[77]

---

[76] D. Martyn Lloyd-Jones, *Studies in the Sermon on the Mount* (Grand Rapids: William B. Eerdmans Publishing Company, 1984), 244.

[77] Ephesians 4:11-15 – "And He gave some as apostles, and some as prophets, and some as evangelists, and some as pastors and teachers, for the equipping of the saints for the work of service, to the building up of the body of Christ; until we all attain to the unity of the faith, and of the knowledge of the Son of God, to a mature man, to the measure of the stature which belongs to the fullness of Christ. As a result, we are no longer to be children, tossed here and there by waves and carried about by every wind of doctrine, by the trickery

3. Train the Church to Share the Ministry (Eph 4:11-12)

Although not all Bible teachers are gifted and equipped to become church elders, all elders are to be teachers. It is not enough that he be able to teach, which is an elder requirement of 1 Timothy 3:2. Serving elders, who lead Christ's church, should be actively involved in the teaching/equipping ministry of the Word. Paul made this clear as he spoke of specifically gifted individuals, who minister God's Word.

> "And He gave some as apostles, and some as prophets, and some as evangelists, and some as pastors and teachers, for the equipping of the saints for the work of service, to the building up of the body of Christ; until we all attain to the unity of the faith, and of the knowledge of the Son of God, to a mature man, to the measure of the stature which belongs to the fullness of Christ." (Eph 4:11-13)

Most Bible scholars agree that when Paul refers to pastors and teachers, he is not delineating two separate groups, but only one: pastor/teachers, or teaching/shepherds.[78] Although no absolute exegetical link can be made from this passage alone, Paul does clearly link them in 1 Timothy 5:17 by saying, "The elders who rule well are to be considered worthy of double honor, especially those who work hard at preaching and teaching."

All pastors should be actively involved in a teaching ministry, and the goal of that teaching is clearly stated in Ephesians 4.

---

of men, by craftiness in deceitful scheming; but speaking the truth in love, we are to grow up in all aspects into Him who is the head, even Christ,"

[78] John MacArthur, Jr, *MacArthur New Testament Commentary: Ephesians* (Chicago: Moody Press, 1986), 143.

Teaching/shepherds should be teaching the Scriptures in such a way as to assist Christians in their spiritual growth and maturity. Paul exhorts shepherds to teach "for the equipping of the saints for the work of service ..." (Eph 4:12). To equip (*katartismos*) means to complete or to restore something to its original useful purpose (i.e., the setting of bones).[79] This is not teaching merely for head knowledge or for personal edification; Paul's goal looks beyond the immediate recipients to the ones they, in turn, will be able to teach and mature. Hebrews 13:20-21 says, "Now the God of peace ... equip (*katartismos*) you in every good thing to do His will, working in us that which is pleasing in His sight, through Jesus Christ, to whom be the glory forever and ever. Amen." Here again, we see that the purpose of teaching is to equip the saints, who in turn will glorify Christ by their maturity and obedience. Paul exhorted Pastor Timothy in this process in 2 Timothy 2:2, "The things which you have heard from me in the presence of many witnesses, entrust these to faithful men who will be able to teach others also." Jesus' last instructions on earth were to "... make disciples of all the nations, baptizing them in the name of the Father and the Son and the Holy Spirit, teaching them to observe all that I commanded you ..." (Matt 28:19-20).

Sadly, many churches hire pastors, expecting them to do all the work of the ministry, and many of them are all too willing to do it. However, this clearly violates Paul's exhortation of Ephesians 4:11-12. Rather than the pastor doing the ministry of one hundred men, it is far better for him to train those hundred men to do the work of the ministry. So rather than elders merely sitting through board meetings making decisions, which guide the direction of the church, they need to be actively involved in

---

[79] Ibid., 152.

the teaching and equipping of the church to share in the work of ministry. Although this is not a new teaching, it is new to many pastors and churches, who need to repent of the *one-man-band* ministry model and embrace the discipleship model of Ephesians 4:11-12.

4. Able to Recognize and the Courage to Refute False Teaching (Titus 1:9-11)

Not only must the elder be able to teach, he must be able to refute (*elegcho*), meaning to expose, convict and reprove those who contradict (*antilego*), meaning to speak against the truth. If the pastor does not have the exegetical tools to mine God's truth, how will he ever recognize and refute false teachers who are contradicting it?

The logical elder qualification progression continues with Paul's warning and exhortation in Titus 1:10-11 where he warns of "... many rebellious men, empty talkers and deceivers ...," and then he commands that they "... must be silenced because they are upsetting whole families, teaching things they should not teach for the sake of sordid gain." The elder must not only know the truth and teach the truth, but he must also have the courage and skill to stand up for the truth in order to silence these false teachers who are upsetting whole families. Shepherds do not just feed the sheep; they beat off the wolves. And sometimes, they get badly chewed in the process, but that is our calling. Real sheep do not attack and chew their shepherds, but God's sheep are sometimes known to join in with the wolves. But in spite of all this, Jesus set the example for all shepherds of God's people who would follow Him, by saying, "I am the good shepherd; the good shepherd lays down His life for the sheep" (John 10:11). This speaks of courage under fire, regardless of the source. Note the clear distinction that He made between someone who is just a hired hand and one who is a true shepherd. A hired hand, "... sees the wolf coming, and leaves the sheep and flees, and the wolf snatches them and scatters them. He flees because he is a hired hand and is not concerned about the sheep" (John 10:12-13).

God's true shepherds do not cut and run when wolves threaten the flock, or just because the wolves do not like them. Pastors must have the courage to stand up against every new wave of false doctrine and practice. He must be willing to even name names in order to clearly identify these errors and those who propagate them.

Paul not only had biblical convictions, but he had the courage of his convictions. He was constantly having to refute and correct false teaching and teachers, but he was never arrogant in his words or ways. He instructed young Pastor Timothy in the way of godly correction, saying,

> The Lord's bond-servant must not be quarrelsome, but be kind to all, able to teach, patient when wronged, with gentleness correcting those who are in opposition, if perhaps God may grant them repentance leading to the knowledge of the truth, and they may come to their senses and escape from the snare of the devil, having been held captive by him to do his will (2 Tim 2:24-26).

Later in this same letter, he gives personal testimony, saying, "I have fought the good fight, I have finished the course, I have kept the faith" (2 Tim 4:7). Paul fought the good fight. This does not mean that he was a pugnacious brawler; rather, it means that he was not quarrelsome, but he was kind to all, and patient when wronged. He was gentle with those who opposed him and his teaching.

As was mentioned earlier, all of us could and should take a lesson from the late Walter Martin. He was not only an authority on false religions and the writer of *Kingdom of the Cults,* but he was a true example of 2 Timothy 2:24-26. For many years, he went head-to-head with cultist leaders from all over the world. And although he would not compromise the truths of Scripture, he never stooped to treating his opponents with disrespect or dishonor. He was a true and living example of biblical knowledge, courage, wisdom, courtesy, and honor, as he spoke the truth in love (Eph 4:15).

5. Shepherd of God's Sheep (Acts 20:28; 1 Pet 5:1-3)

Paul exhorted the Ephesian elders, "Be on guard for yourselves and for all the flock, among which the Holy Spirit has made you overseers, to shepherd the church of God which He purchased with His own blood" (Acts 20:28). The Bible often refers to God's people as sheep in need of a shepherd. Paul picks up this metaphor when speaking of elders as those who would shepherd (*poimnion*) Christ's sheep.[80] Where the title elder speaks of godly wisdom and spiritual maturity, shepherd or pastor speaks of the love and leadership aspects of those who would care for God's flock. Pastors must remember that these are not his sheep; they belong to Christ, who purchased them with His own blood. As God's overseer, (Titus 1:7) the shepherd watches over that which belongs to another. First Peter 2:25 gives these comforting words, "For you were continually straying like sheep, but now you have returned to the Shepherd (*Poimen*) and Guardian of your souls." Jesus is the good Shepherd (John 10:11,14), who both knows His sheep and lays down His life for

---

[80] John MacArthur, Jr, *MacArthur New Testament Commentary: Acts 13-28* (Chicago: Moody Press, 1996), 224.

them. Elders serve as under-shepherds as they themselves follow their good Shepherd.

One of the many problems with sheep is that they do not know the difference between noxious weeds and healthy food, so the shepherd must be constantly vigilant to pull the weeds as he prepares their pasture. And so it is with God's sheep, especially the young ones. They are prone to feed on false doctrines that will either infect and/or starve them. God spoke against the leaders of Israel, and His words should be shouted again today concerning those who fail to faithfully shepherd Christ's church.

> Then the word of the LORD came to me saying, "Son of man, prophesy against the shepherds of Israel. Prophesy and say to those shepherds, Thus says the Lord GOD, 'Woe, shepherds of Israel who have been feeding themselves! Should not the shepherds feed the flock? You eat the fat and clothe yourselves with the wool, you slaughter the fat sheep without feeding the flock. Those who are sickly you have not strengthened, the diseased you have not healed, the broken you have not bound up, the scattered you have not brought back, nor have you sought for the lost; but with force and with severity you have dominated them. They were scattered for lack of a shepherd, and they became food for every beast of the field and were scattered.'" (Ezek 34:1-5).

Peter made it clear that Christians must be nourished by God's Word, "... like newborn babies, long for the pure milk of the word, so that by it you may grow in respect to salvation" (1 Pet 2:2).

Peter referred to himself as an elder and saw the necessity of exhorting his fellow elders concerning the manner in which they should shepherd God's sheep.

> ... I exhort the elders among you, as your fellow elder and witness of the sufferings of Christ, and a partaker also of the glory that is to be revealed, shepherd the flock of God among you, exercising oversight not under compulsion, but voluntarily, according to the will of God; and not for sordid gain, but with eagerness; nor yet as lording it over those allotted to your charge, but proving to be examples to the flock. And when the Chief Shepherd appears, you will receive the unfading crown of glory (1 Pet 5:1-4).

As Peter commands elders to shepherd the flock of God, he also reminds them to do it voluntarily, faithfully, unselfishly, and eagerly, even as he warns them against lording it over those allotted to their charge. Cattle are typically driven with a bullwhip, but sheep must be led. If one tries to drive them like cattle, they scatter in every direction. Wise shepherds also understand that they cannot treat all the sheep the same; each one has special individual needs that he must lovingly understand and care for. Paul urged the Thessalonian church to, "... admonish (*noutheteo*) the unruly, encourage the fainthearted, help the weak, be patient with everyone" (1 Thess 5:14).

God's shepherds lead by example, always seeking to please the Chief Shepherd, knowing that they will give account for the manner in which they led and cared for His blood-bought sheep. Many pastors today would do well to remember that the church does not exist to meet their needs. Quite the contrary, shepherds are to spend and be spent as they lovingly lead and gently care for the needs of God's sheep.

Healthy flocks do not just happen overnight; they are the result of years of careful and wise leadership. Wise elders understand that they cannot shepherd from afar; they must be close to God's sheep if they are truly going to lead them in paths of righteousness. Godly shepherds lead and feed in public and in private. The excellent exposition of the Word to the church as a whole is essential for a healthy flock. However, loving shepherds do not shepherd from afar. They have to get their hands, as it were, down into the wool, and this takes lots of time and personal contact. Good shepherds not only know the names of God's sheep, but they go to great efforts to know them personally. This is why it takes more than one qualified elder to have a healthy church. They must be available to visit and pray for the sick, help the weak, counsel, comfort, bear burdens, marry, and bury. Large churches need to work at being small, so that individuals are not lost in the crowd, where there are enough shepherds to reach out and care for them individually. Caring shepherds serve long hours to remain near and dear to God's sheep. They feed and care for the strong and the weak, the healthy and the sick, the lost and the found. Hebrews 13:17 speaks of shepherds as the ones who "... keep watch over your souls as those who will give an account ..." Therefore, they must always be vigilant, never forgetting that it is God's flock that he tends.[81]

Biblical counseling by elders is personal by nature. But some pastors, who say that they love the church, would rather be in their studies. One prominent but shortsighted pastor of a large church scoffed at the very thought of his church ever needing a trained biblical counselor on the pastoral staff, saying,

---

[81] Strauch, op. cit., 16.

> I do all my counseling from the pulpit; that is all the people need. Several years ago, we got us one of those "biblical counselors," and all of the sudden we had a church full of people with problems. I got rid of the counselor, and the problems went away!

Were the truth told, the problems did not go away; they merely went back underground, buried in the hearts of hurting sheep, who had no shepherds to care for them. Sadly, this is how many churches operate. Even if they do not brazenly say so, the results are the same. As necessary as systematic expository preaching is to the overall health of the flock, it will never take the place of personal loving contact with God's sheep. For example, preachers need to realize that it may be years before they get back to sermons previously taught in Ephesians 5 and 6 dealing with the Holy Spirit-controlled family. Husbands and wives, fathers, mothers, and children often need individualized help, nurture, encouragement, instruction, application, and personal accountability.

Parenthetically, it is essential to remember that elders must be committed to "... the equipping of the church for the work of service ..." (Eph 4:11-12). Nowhere is this more true than in the area of biblical counseling. Paul commended the church at Rome saying, "And concerning you, my brethren, I myself also am convinced that you yourselves are full of goodness, filled with all knowledge and able also to admonish (noutheteo) one another" (Rom 15:14). It should be noted here that the Apostle was not speaking to only a few highly trained biblical counselors. He was speaking to the entire church, who knew the Word of God and how to minister it in the counseling of one another. This is why the New Testament never refers to the "spiritual gift of counseling," because according to Paul, every Christian is to participate in it.

The writer of Hebrews exhorted all Christians, not just a few 'gifted' biblical counselors to, "... encourage one another day after day, as long as it is still called 'Today,' so that none of you will be hardened by the deceitfulness of sin" (Hebrews 3:13). But sadly, very few pastors today participate in this biblically mandated ministry of the local church. They often say things like, "I am not gifted in this area," or "I don't have any training," or "I just don't have time." But in the end, these are all just excuses which bear no biblical support. So rather than just sending God's sheep out to the secular wolves or to so-called "Christian" counseling centers, which have no accountability to the church and who are often even hostile to it, faithful shepherds must take the lead by counseling and training other biblical counselors to share in the work of the ministry under the purview of the local church.

The Faith Baptist Church of Lafayette, Indiana, is just such a church, not only committed to biblical counseling, but to the training of biblical counselors. Lloyd Jonas, who served there as one of their pastors, remarked, "Because this entire church is so well taught in the Word and in biblical counseling, it is rare for any of its members to need to seek pastoral counsel. It is fully equipped with laymen who are able to carry this ministry in most cases."

Shepherds not only lead and feed the sheep and beat off wolves, sometimes they even need to protect the flock from themselves, as they are prone to go astray, either following wolves dressed up like shepherds or merely following after their own fleshly ideas. Paul warned the Ephesians elders concerning their need to be faithful shepherds once he was gone:

> I know that after my departure savage wolves will come in among you, not sparing the flock; and from among your own selves men will arise, speaking perverse things, to draw away the disciples after them. Therefore be on the alert, remembering that night and day for a period of three years I did not cease to admonish (*noutheteo*) each one with tears (Acts 20:29-31).

Paul not only taught the church as a whole, but he admonished *(noutheteo)* (i.e., counseled) them individually with tears, all the while knowing that their worst enemies would eventually rise up from among their so-called brethren, some of the very men he had discipled and appointed to be elders.

Not only must shepherds be aware of potential wolves arising from within the flock, they must also be watchful of those on the outside who would seek to infiltrate and pollute them with humanistic thinking, turning God's sheep away from the all-sufficient Word of God. Spiritual alertness includes not only understanding the nature and needs of sheep, but the shepherd must also be a student of predators. He must know the times and ways in which they usually attack. As a shepherd lamented over his torn lambs, a bystander asked him why none of the mature sheep had been attacked. To which he responded, "Wolves rarely bother with sheep when there are lambs to be had." God's shepherds must be aware of how the enemy seeks to capture and pervert our youth, and he must be able to stand firm with biblical conviction to counter attractive attacks with truth. Sadly, many churches today are more interested in numerical growth than spiritual growth, so they invite in any number of cleverly-disguised worldly schemes to boost numbers and dollars, not realizing that they will actually stunt their spiritual growth as they bring ruin and destruction from within. Simply put, faithful shepherds must be aware of the world's constant efforts to lower the moral standards of God's people.

One pastor, who had done an exemplary job of caring for his aged mother-in-law over a period of seven years, agreed to have her basic life supports of nutrition and hydration taken away shortly after she had a stroke. She was not in a coma. In fact, she was fully aware of her circumstances and surroundings. But a humanistic doctor convinced him that it was best to hasten her death, rather than allowing her to die of natural causes. As soon as this biblically indefensible decision was made, some of the family members reached out to me for help. Although I attempted to biblically admonish this pastor, even bringing in expert medical information to educate him concerning the physical horrors of what he was doing to his mother-in-law, I was unsuccessful. So he and the doctors tortured and killed her with starvation and dehydration. In the conversations leading up to her death, it became quite apparent that this pastor was more concerned about preserving her estate, not giving it all to the doctors, than he was with shepherding and caring for the life that was in his hands. Well did Isaiah rebuke the false shepherds of his day, "... the dogs are greedy, they are not satisfied ... they are shepherds who have no understanding; they have all turned to their own way, each one to his unjust gain ..." (Isa 56:11). Needless to say, others in his flock were watching and would likely follow his godless example.

Philip Keller summarized the role and heart of a shepherd, who follows after the good Shepherd, saying, "All the care, all the work, all the alert watchfulness, all the skill, all the concern, all the self-sacrifice are born of His love – the love of One who loves His sheep, loves His work, loves His role as a Shepherd."[82]

6. Willing and Able to Exhort Fellow Elders (Gal 2:11-21)

Because church elders are by definition the leaders of the church, they must deal personally with men and issues on their own board. That is, they must have the courage to exhort and/or confront one another regarding biblically-defined sin. In Galatians 2:11-21, we have the account of Paul rebuking Peter.

> But when Cephas came to Antioch, I opposed him to his face, because he stood condemned. For prior to the coming of certain men from James, he used to eat with the Gentiles; but when they came, he began to withdraw and hold himself aloof, fearing the party of the circumcision. The rest of the Jews joined him in hypocrisy, with the result that even Barnabas was carried away by their hypocrisy. But when I saw that they were not straightforward about the truth of the gospel, I said to Cephas in the presence of all, 'If you, being a Jew, live like the Gentiles and not like the Jews, how is it that you compel the Gentiles to live like Jews? ...'

We know that Peter must have repented because he continued in ministry without any further mention of the matter. Although God holds elders to a high standard, this necessary work of loving confrontation (Eph 4:15) is essential if the body of Christ is to remain healthy. In fact, the writer of Hebrews makes it clear that this type of healthy one-on-one ministry should be normal among Christians, even on a daily basis. "But encourage

---

[82] Philip Keller, *A Shepherd Looks at the 23rd Psalm* (Grand Rapids: Zondervan Publishing House, 1970), 130.

one another day after day, as long as it is still called 'Today,' so that none of you will be hardened by the deceitfulness of sin" (Heb 3:13). And the church discipline process of Matthew 18:15-17[83] is not reserved for the non-elders of the church; it includes everyone, because anyone, including elders, can succumb to the hardening influence of sin. When pastors sin, they must be held biblically accountable, even as the rest of the of the church; and if they fail to repent, they too must be dealt with in a biblical fashion. Paul makes this clear in 1 Timothy 5:20-21, "Those (elders) who continue in sin, rebuke in the presence of all, so that the rest also will be fearful of sinning. I solemnly charge you in the presence of God and of Christ Jesus and of His chosen angels, to maintain these principles without bias, doing nothing in a spirit of partiality." The church needs to be assured that no matter who you are, unrepentant sin will be biblically confronted.

Because of the very nature of the shepherd/sheep relationship, laymen will be hesitant to confront their pastors, which is all the more reason for elders to be holding one another to high biblical standards. As has been previously mentioned, biblically-qualified elders, whether paid or unpaid, whether they be part-time or full-time in their ministry to the church, all serve as peers; and as such, they must hold each other accountable. Some have referred to them as a "Council of Equals."[84] The preaching and/or senior pastor must never be considered as the

---

[83] Matthew 18:15-17 – "If your brother sins, go and show him his fault in private; if he listens to you, you have won your brother. But if he does not listen to you, take one or two more with you, so that by the mouth of two or three witnesses every fact may be confirmed. If he refuses to listen to them, tell it to the church; and if he refuses to listen even to the church, let him be to you as a Gentile and a tax collector."

[84] Strauch, op. cit., 39.

head elder or the head of the church. Christ alone is the Head of His Church.

The pastor must never use his position in the ministry as a means to either bully the other elders into accepting his ideas, or to shield himself from legitimate biblical criticism. However, this is often the case. When Peter was caught and confronted with his sin, he repented, but many sinning pastors today attempt to use their position, prestige, and influence to short-circuit what has come to be known as: "The Matthew 18 Process." In such cases, his fellow elders must hold him accountable as they would any other member of the church, and if necessary, his unrepentance must be confronted before the entire church. But all too often, his sins are merely explained away or swept under the carpet, and his fellow elders, who may have tried to expose him, are either fired or intimidated out of the church. In such cases, a sinning pastor becomes hardened in his sin as he becomes more and more brazen in exerting his unbalanced authority. Elders must be above reproach, but they are never to see themselves as being above the scrutiny of God's Word or their fellow elders.

CHAPTER 3

BIBLICAL PATTERN FOR RECOGNIZING AND INSTALLING ELDERS

When it comes to finding a truly absolute biblical pattern for recognizing and installing elders, the church today cannot do so because all the first elders were Apostles, chosen directly by Christ. As the church grew geographically, elders like Timothy and Titus were appointed by an existing elder, Paul. Since we no longer have any clear lineage of apostolic ecclesiastical authority, the church today must apply all of the aforementioned biblical qualifications to anyone who would aspire to this leadership position, and that only after he has fully and honestly examined himself.

One of the best, albeit imperfect, means of recognizing those whom God has called out for pastoral service is that of an ordination council. In this model, seasoned, mature, and godly men from other like-minded churches gather to examine a potential candidate. In point of fact, they are not the ones who ordain the man; their purpose is only to, as best as humanly possible, determine whether or not God has called him to serve as an elder in Christ's church. Typically, many hours are spent studying the candidate's doctrinal statement and asking him clarification questions as to his theology. Any responsible council will also seek to ask the hard questions about his personal and family life. They will attempt to determine the scope and success of the ministries, in which he has been involved as a laymen. Often, practical questions regarding the typical problems of pastoral ministry will be asked to test the candidate concerning his wisdom and ability to think biblically to Christ-honoring solutions, which will enable him to navigate the church through the often-troubled waters of body life. After all the questions have been asked and answered, and after much prayer, the council will discuss the candidate together, seeking to come to a unanimous sense of his call to the ministry. Their findings will typically come in one of three answers: First, they may agree that the candidate is called and ready to enter the pastoral ministry. Second, they may believe that he is called, but he is not yet mature enough in his faith and/or theology and wisdom to enter the ministry at this time. In such cases, they will attempt to assist and instruct the candidate in the specific areas that he needs to develop before he can serve as a pastor. And Third, the council may agree that he is not called and therefore is not qualified to serve as an elder. This last decision is certainly difficult, but men of integrity must occasionally make it. In these cases, the rejected candidate will likely need wise biblical counseling, both to help him accept their findings and to assist him in knowing where he needs to grow and how he can still serve the church as a layman. Clearly, all of their findings are not absolute, but if they are honest, mature, and honorable men, in most situations, time will prove them to have been correct.

Since there is no biblical difference between elder/pastors who serve the church full-time vocationally and elder/pastors who make their living outside the church, there should be similar methods of determining God's calling for all of them. However, most often, full-time pastors receive a far closer scrutiny than their non-vocational counterparts, with the result being that many unqualified men find their way into church leadership, and that to the harm of Christ's church. Since any given local church will rarely rise above the moral character and biblical wisdom of its leaders, the careful choosing of elders is foundational to the welfare of the church, showing fruit for generations to come.

CHAPTER 4

BIBLICAL COUNSELING OF THOSE WHO DESIRE TO BECOME ELDERS

Although it should be self-evident that each of the aforementioned qualifications are in themselves biblical counseling exhortations and admonitions, there are still several specific matters that need to be addressed which will provide a clear and practical roadmap to any potential elder candidate.

As has been previously stated, candidates for church leadership must be examined by impartial biblically-qualified elders to determine, as far as humanly possible, whether or not they meet these minimum standards. Although Paul was speaking specifically to deacons in 1 Timothy 3:10, "These men must also first be tested ..." the context would clearly apply to the testing of elder candidates as well. A man must realize that merely believing he is biblically qualified does not necessarily make it so.

For example, one newly-baptized convert told his pastor that he wanted to join the church and become a deacon (that church did not have elders). He was a wealthy leader in his community and wrongly assumed that he should be invited automatically into church leadership. When the pastor pointed out to him that he was biblically disqualified because he was a new convert, and that his current third marriage was on very shaky ground, the man became angry saying, "Well, if I can't join the church and become a deacon immediately, then I'll go somewhere else where I can." Clearly, his words and attitude revealed far more than these two biblical disqualifications, and that is what the testing process is all about. It is intended to both weed out those who are disqualified, while at the same time affirming those who are.

As a candidate goes through the list personally and/or with the church elders, there will often be disqualifying areas of his life that are exposed for the first time. Although no elder can claim perfection concerning any of these qualifications (for we must all be growing by the grace of God until the day we die), these minimal standards must be firmly nailed planks in his moral character and practical knowledge of the Word. Wise pastoral/mentors must be able and willing to invest the time and energy in leading such men to maturity in Christ and eventual leadership in the church. Depending on the type of biblical disqualification (temporary or permanent), and assuming that the disqualified candidate is willing, discipling elders must be prepared to minister real hope and the practical help of biblical counseling to the man, so that he may become an honor to God and useful to the church, even if it is not in a leadership position.

Although there is some disagreement among Christian leaders today as to whether or not a man can and should be permanently disqualified for elder leadership because of certain heinous sins, most biblical scholars agree that these permanent disqualifications do exist. However, as one goes down through the list, he should easily see that the failure to achieve most of the biblical standards need not be permanent. He can repent, grow, demonstrate faithfulness, and eventually be ordained to an elder role. However, there are some sinful behaviors and actions that will permanently disqualify a man. A lack of personal moral discipline, as would be evidenced by adultery or other lewd and lascivious acts, speaks of deep and lasting defects to a man's character. Although there can be no question as to whether or not the man can repent and receive forgiveness and restoration in his relationship to Christ and the church, there will always be a cloud of doubt over him.

There are some who mistakenly maintain that God treats all sin the same by quoting, "... the blood of Jesus ... cleanses us from all sin" (1 John 1:7). They then ask, "Who are we to hold a man's sin against him, when God has forgiven?" However, the Bible is clear that God does not treat all sin the same. Although there are some common aspects of sin that have the same effect upon us all, as demonstrated in Isaiah 59:2, "But your iniquities have made a separation between you and your God, and your sins have hidden His face from you so that He does not hear," there are still some significant differences. The biblical point that the counselor must make clear is that forgiveness is not, nor was it ever, at issue. The Bible assures us that God will forgive sin, any and all sin, when we come to Him in repentant faith. Note the superlative of 1 John 1:7, where the Apostle declares "... the blood of Jesus His Son cleanses us from all sin." So the problem is not forgiveness, but rather it is effectiveness; namely, can a man, after being involved in any of the aforementioned sexual sins, ever have a trustworthy effective pastoral/elder ministry?

For example, if a star baseball pitcher gets drunk after a game, plows his car into a tree, and wakes up in the hospital with his pitching arm, shoulder, and elbow shattered, will he ever pitch again? The answer is, "No." But can he still be of some use to the team? The answer is, "Yes." Although there are other crucial and important players on the team, winning clubs are all about outstanding pitchers. And so it is with the church, whose members will rarely rise above the moral character of their pastors. Effective God-honoring ministry rightly centers around godly leaders, and that is why God set the moral bar so high. But when a man fails this biblical moral test, and then is restored back into the leadership ministry that he once knew, it not only lowers the moral standard for everyone else in the church, but it also brings shame and reproach upon Christ and the church before an unbelieving world. King Solomon understood this matter well, and he exhorted his son accordingly. "The one who commits adultery with a woman is lacking sense; he who would destroy himself does it. Wounds and disgrace he will find, and his reproach will not be blotted out" (Proverbs 6:32-33). Forgiveness yes -- effectiveness no.

Some who vehemently disagree with the biblical standard and the aforementioned analogy will cite the repentance and restoration of King David, who committed adultery, murder, and a lying cover-up. Yet upon his confession and repentance, God not only allowed him to live, but he was allowed to remain on as the King of Israel. However, David was neither an Old Testament priest, nor was he a New Testament pastor. Therefore, God's sovereign choice to keep him in office can bear no exegetical comparison with fallen elders today.

Even a godly chosen man of God like Paul made it clear that he lived with the understanding that he too was not exempt from measuring up to the biblical standards that he commanded others to keep. It appears that Paul may have been a sports fan of what was known then as the Isthmian Games.[1] Like the Olympics, these were amateur athletes who participated for the

---

[1] John MacArthur, Jr, *MacArthur New Testament Commentary: 1 Corinthians* (Chicago: Moody Press, 1984), 215.

love of the sport and the glory that winning a *perishable wreath* would bring. He wrote,

> Everyone who competes in the games exercises self-control in all things. They then do it to receive a perishable wreath, but we an imperishable. Therefore I run in such a way, as not without aim; I box in such a way, as not beating the air; but I discipline my body and make it my slave, so that, after I have preached to others, I myself will not be disqualified (1 Cor 9:25-27).

In this text, he draws spiritual truth from a boxing metaphor. Even as a winning boxer would have to discipline his body, Paul did the same. This discipline (*hupopiazo*) was so severe that it carried with it the meaning of hitting oneself to the point of being black and blue. Although Paul was certainly not advocating self-mutilation, he was asserting that one's body needed to be brought under control, even to the point of withdrawing personal rights or liberties, as was the case with a Roman slave (*doulagogeo*).[2] And why did Paul so discipline himself? He continues to draw from the same metaphor of the Isthmian Games. Like in today's Olympics, in order for a man to be able to participate in the games, he had to qualify; and without such prequalifications, he would not even be able to run, let alone win. However, even after he qualified, he was still required to participate according to the rules; and if it was found out that he cheated, he was disqualified. Paul lived knowing that even he could become disqualified (*adokimos*), one who was a rejected castaway.

---

[2] Idem.

Although Paul's salvation was never at issue in this illustration, effective service for Christ and His church certainly was. Previously, he made it clear that sexual sin was in a class all by itself. He commanded and then made this appeal: "Flee immorality. Every other sin that a man commits is outside the body, but the immoral man sins against his own body. Or do you not know that your body is a temple of the Holy Spirit who is in you, whom you have from God, and that you are not your own?" (1 Cor 6:18-19). The sexual relationship goes to the deepest part of a man's soul, either for the glory and honor of God or for the sinful gratification of self. Although Christians can and do sin, those who are immoral will never be the same again. Even though God's forgiveness is freely offered and restoration with his wife is possible, the cloud of distrust will never leave him. Again, Proverbs 6:32-33 says it plainly: "The one who commits adultery with a woman is lacking sense; he who would destroy himself does it. Wounds and disgrace he will find, and his reproach will not be blotted out." Unlike the thief, there is no way that he can ever make restitution for this sin and therefore, he can never again be above reproach (1 Tim 3:2). Although he can and must be biblically counseled to become a one-woman man (1 Tim 3:2), he will never be able to wipe out the stain of his past.

Many otherwise orthodox churches today wrongly see moral failure in their leadership as some sort of badge of honor to the grace of God, rather than what it actually is, a blight on Christ and His church. It has almost become vogue in some circles to have a fallen or unbiblically divorced pastor. Church members say things like, "Because he is just like us, now our pastor can really understand and empathize with us and our problems." Although this false reasoning may sound good, it is, at best, unbiblical, corrupt, and shortsighted thinking because it effectively lowers the bar of God's absolute moral standards for everyone, leaving a comfortable, calloused, and crippled church.

Unfortunately, hardly any churches practice the restorative grace of "The Matthew 18 Process" today. Their stated reasons usually boil down to the fear lawsuits, and the fear that they will be accused of being unloving, judgmental, and unforgiving, which they say will result in people leaving the church in droves. And yet, we would all do well to understand and remember that Jesus' first instructions to His church dealt with the 4-Step "Matthew 18 Process."

Paul addressed this certainty as he rebuked the Corinthians for their refusal to discipline a sexually immoral man in their church, saying, "Your boasting is not good. Do you not know that a little leaven leavens the whole lump of dough? Clean out the old leaven so that you may be a new lump ..." (1 Cor 5:6-7). All Christians, but especially church leaders, must remember that the church belongs to Christ and as such, He alone has the right to set the standards for its leadership, and no one dares lower them for any reason.

Three couples once came to me for counseling concerning a well-known leader in their church who had divorced his wife without biblical cause and was presently living with another woman in the church. After being instructed, the men began going through the biblical steps of Matthew 18:15-17. At each point, they were rebuffed, and so they finally went to the church elders, expecting them to follow through. However, they were not prepared for the answer they received, where the pastor declared, "If we deal with this situation, as the Bible says, where will it all end?" Apparently, these men knew that immorality was rampant in the church, and this individual offender was only the tip of the iceberg. Most of the church had become comfortable in their sinning, and the elders had neither the conviction, character, nor courage to do anything about it. All three of those couples soon left that church in search of one that honored God and His Word and where the elders were men of integrity.

In such cases, where God's moral standard for church leaders has been effectively, albeit sinfully, lowered, David is often used as an example of one who was immoral and yet was allowed to remain on as Israel's king. They quote passages like: "David did what was right in the sight of the LORD, and had not turned aside from anything that He commanded him all the days of his life, except in the case of Uriah the Hittite" (1 Kgs 15:5), and "... The LORD has sought out for Himself a man after His own heart, and the LORD has appointed him as ruler over His people ..." (1 Sam 13:14). In pointing out the error of such applications, it is necessary to note again that King David was neither a priest nor a pastor. Although both David and Solomon were greatly blessed and used by God, they were never freed from the stigma of their immorality. "Did not Solomon king of Israel sin regarding these things? Yet ... he was loved by his God ... nevertheless the foreign women caused even him to sin" (Neh 13:26).[3]

Even though 1 John 1:9 is still in the Book, morally corrupt elders must be exposed, disciplined, and permanently removed from the ministry. However, if and when repentance and confession is made and forgiveness sought, spiritual restoration to fellowship with the church must be as public as the discipline. However, restoration to the pastoral ministry as an elder is biblically forbidden.[4]

---

[3] John MacArthur, Jr, *MacArthur New Testament Commentary: Titus* (Chicago: Moody Press, 1996), 29.

[4] Ibid., 18-19.

CHAPTER 5

BIBLICAL TREATMENT OF CHURCH ELDERS BY THE CONGREGATION

So far, the focus has been on the biblical qualifications of those who would lead Christ's church. The Bible not only instructs the church in the qualifying and recognizing of these men, but it also makes strong exhortations as to their treatment by the congregation.

As Paul concluded his first letter to the Thessalonian church, he instructed them regarding the treatment of their elders by saying "... we request of you, brethren, that you appreciate those who diligently labor among you, and have charge over you in the Lord and give you instruction, and that you esteem them very highly in love because of their work ..." (1 Thess 5:12-13). To hold one in high esteem (*hegeomai*), means to recognize and appreciate his position of authority. Paul used it to refer to master/slave relationship in 1 Timothy 6:1. It was also used often in reference to considering all the facts in order to render a judgment (Jas 1:2). Putting these two ideas together as they relate to the treatment of elders, once the church comes to a biblical understanding of the lofty character and ministry requirements of their elders, they in turn should hold them in highest honor. Paul instructed Timothy, and by extension the entire Ephesian church, saying, "The elders who rule well are to be considered worthy of double honor (*time*), especially those who work hard at preaching and teaching. For the Scripture says, 'You shall not muzzle the ox while he is threshing,' and 'The laborer is worthy of his wages'" (1 Tim 5:17-18). Honor (*time*) is most often used in the New Testament to refer to a payment or price. The following verse makes it abundantly clear that Paul is speaking about paying the pastor. And because those who rule well and work hard at preaching and teaching were especially valuable to the well-being of the church, they were "worthy of double honor." In other words, they should be well paid.[1] Paul's reference to not muzzling the ox was a quotation from the Old Testament law, where God instructed His people concerning the proper treatment of the animal, which was working so that they could have food. The obvious point was, if God cares about the proper treatment of a working animal, how much more does he care about the welfare of His undershepherds who labor in the care of His sheep. But sadly, because many churches do not appreciate their vocational elders, they pay them accordingly. To the extent that these elders devote themselves to the nurture and shepherding of the church, the church should be committing itself to supporting (paying) those who lead and care for it.

Hebrews 13:17 exhorts believers to, "Obey (*peitho*) your leaders and submit (*hupeiko*) to them, for they keep watch over your souls as those who will give an account. Let them do this with joy and not with grief, for this would be unprofitable for you." To obey (*peitho*), means to trust, to yield, or put confidence in. Because these men must be of the highest moral and spiritual caliber, they are worthy of the church's confidence and trust;

---

[1] John MacArthur, Jr, *MacArthur New Testament Commentary: 1 Timothy* (Chicago: Moody Press, 1995), 219.

therefore, the church is exhorted to submit (*hupeiko*) to them. Of course, this submission is not blind obedience. Wise elders, like wise parents, demonstrate the biblical basis for their instructions. Such understanding makes submitting attractive. Because there is enough grief for shepherds as they minister to the day-to-day needs and burdens of the flock, the writer encourages the church by saying that their godly responses to their elders will bring them joy rather than needless sorrow.

Once the honor and payment issues had been addressed, Paul continues with a practical application in 1 Timothy 5:19. If the church was expressing the proper honor and high esteem for their biblically-qualified pastors, then they would also "... not receive an accusation against an elder except on the basis of two or three witnesses." Although the elder is not exempted from the church discipline process of Matthew 18:15-17 and 1 Timothy 5:20, he must be shielded from the frivolous or malicious accusations of others.[2] That said, the pastor must guard himself against foolish and/or careless words or actions, which could bring shame upon the name of Christ and His church, and permanently disqualify him from the ministry. And as I have said previously, the elder must remember that he need not be guilty; he only has to be undefendable, (his word against hers). Remember "The Billy Graham Rule."

On a very practical note, Amy Carmichael was a pioneer missionary to the people of India for 55 years. She understood first-hand, the devastation and ruin that gossip and slander among missionaries can bring to God's work. And so, she would teach the young missionaries who came to serve with her, "Speak to, not about! — Speak **to**, not **about**!"

---

[2] MacArthur, op. cit., 222.

Simply put, if you have something worth saying, speak **to** the person, not **about** them! So many of the problems that churches suffer, would never happen, if we would just follow these simple words, "Speak **to**, not **about**!" Parents, teach your children by your instruction and by your example. "Speak **to**, not **about**!" And this especially applies to the beloved pastors and elders who serve your church. Speak to them, not about them. Assuming that these men meet the biblical qualifications for the office, you will discover that they are very approachable, that they will listen to you carefully, and respond lovingly. But if you go home each Sunday, and eat "Roast Pastor" at lunch, don't be surprised when your kids hit their teen years, and they want nothing to do with you, or your church.

James 1:26 says, "If anyone thinks himself to be religious, and yet does not bridle his tongue but deceives his own heart, this man's religion is worthless." Nowhere is the link between genuine faith and God-honoring works seen more clearly than in our speech. Words have great power, both for good, or for evil.

Jesus said, "For out of the heart come evil thoughts, murders, adulteries, fornications, thefts, false witness, and slanders" (Matthew 15:19). And yet Solomon declared, "Like apples of gold in settings of silver, is a word spoken, in right circumstances. Like an earring of gold, and an ornament of fine gold, is a wise reprover, to a listening ear" (Proverbs 25:11-12).

What is one of the first things that we do, if we are not feeling well? We take our temperature to determine if we have a fever, which is usually the first indication that we are sick. Just like a thermometer will help to measure the condition of our physical health, so too, our use of words will measure the condition of our spiritual health. Although the writers of the New Testament were concerned about theology, they would all agree that right theology, without a Holy Spirit-controlled tongue, is utterly worthless.

"So also the tongue is a small part of the body, and yet it boasts of great things. See how great a forest is set aflame by such a small fire! And the tongue is a fire, the very world of iniquity; the tongue is set among our members as that which defiles the entire body, and sets on fire the course of our life, and is set on fire by hell." (James 3:5-8)

It only takes a small spark, or a match to start a devastating fire that will destroy both property and lives. Now here is the amazing thing about fire. It will reproduce itself as long as there is fuel to burn. Fire feeds on itself, and it is never satisfied. The Chicago fire of 1871 started in a barn when Mrs. O Leary's cow kicked over a lantern. And before the fire was brought under control, it had destroyed over 17,000 buildings, killed 300 people, and left 125,000 people homeless. But this is nothing, when compared to the destruction that can be caused by the tongue. When the fire danger is high, burning is prohibited; and the Word of God holds up a perpetual prohibition sign that says, "No burning today," and the Holy Spirit is the forest ranger.

On a very personal note, I want to tell you about my dear friend, *William*, who has been in Heaven for many years, but before he died, he gave me permission to share his story. *William* and his wife were founding members of the church where I pastored for almost 20 years. One day he and his wife just quit coming, and they refused to tell me why they had left. But twelve years later, after *William's* wife had died, he and his new wife showed up one morning for church. And as I visited with them later that next week, I asked if he was finally willing to tell me what caused him to leave his beloved church so many years before. After pausing for a long moment, He said, "Someone told me that you believed in, no divorce, and no remarriage, for any reason, ever!" Now *William's* wife had divorced her previous husband, because he had deserted her and their young child, never to be heard from again. So when *William* heard what he thought were my beliefs on divorce and remarriage, instead of coming to me personally to check it out, he assumed that he and his wife were not welcome, so they left. When I told him that he had been misinformed, and that I did not believe or teach these things, he hung his head in deep sorrow. After a long pause he moaned with unbridled sadness, "I have been out of my beloved church for 12 years because I believed a lie? Look at me, I'm 90 years old, and I have nothing left to give."

Thankfully, he was wrong, and for the next three years, *William*, was a wonderful example of God's love and kindness to us all, and even though I buried him, I will never forget him. But what a shame! Even though confession was made and forgiveness was eagerly granted, I could not give back the years that my dear friend had lost. What destruction and sorrow was done by those who gossiped and slandered, and that without ever asking me to clarify my biblical teaching on divorce and remarriage.

I believe that the tongue has that capacity to do more harm, or good, than any other part of our body. Evil words are like bullets, and just like it is impossible to un-shoot a gun, you cannot un-say gossip or slanderous words. All that can be done in such cases is to repent, seek forgiveness of the ones that were hurt, and then attempt to undo the damage.

The well-known story is told about a woman who had destroyed the reputation of a pastor by her gossiping and slander, and when she could not live with her guilty conscience any longer, she went to him and confessed that she was the one who had started all the rumors. Through her tears she begged for his forgiveness and promised to do whatever it would take to undo the damage she had caused. Her pastor graciously forgave her, and then he instructed her to go up on the hill behind the church, where she was to rip open a feather pillow and scatter the feathers out on the ground. And once this was done, she was to report back for further instructions. Although this seemed to be a rather strange assignment, she followed his instructions to the letter. Once the task was completed, she reported back to her pastor, who then told her, "Now go back up there and pick up all the feathers!" In utter consternation she wailed, "But Pastor, certainly you know how the wind blows up there. By now the feathers will have blown everywhere. I might be able to pick up some of them, but most of them will be gone!" To which he answered, "And so it is with your gossip and slander. Although I appreciate the fact that you have sought my forgiveness, and you should attempt to confess what you have done to all those you have spoken to, there is no way for you to undo all the damage you have done to me and to the reputation of this church."

On a more positive note, as we consider the Biblical Treatment of Church Elders By the Congregation, most of these men are like policemen and firemen. No one ever calls the police or fire departments to tell them that they are having a great day, and few ever call to express appreciation for the work that they do. When we call the police or fire hall, it is because we have a 911 situation. And so it is for most us those who serve as elders. So many of the communications we receive are either complaints or 911 calls. Clearly, such calls are part of the elder's job description, but how good and appropriate it is for your pastors to hear your appreciation as well.

As I close this chapter, let's all make King David's prayer our own: "Let the words of my mouth and the meditation of my heart be acceptable in Your sight, O LORD, my rock and my Redeemer" (Psalm 19:14).

CHAPTER 6

BIBLICAL COUNSELING AND THE PROCESS OF CHURCH DISCIPLINE

As illustrated previously, there will be cases where someone in the church will come to believe that either a current elder or an elder candidate is biblically disqualified. In such cases, the Bible gives clear instructions as to how he must proceed.

> Do not judge so that you will not be judged. For in the way you judge, you will be judged; and by your standard of measure, it will be measured to you. Why do you look at the speck that is in your brother's eye, but do not notice the log that is in your own eye? Or how can you say to your brother, 'Let me take the speck out of your eye,' and behold, the log is in your own eye? You hypocrite, first take the log out of your own eye, and then you will see clearly to take the speck out of your brother's eye. (Matthew 7:1-5)

Matthew 7:1, "Do not judge so that you will not be judged..." is one of the most quoted and misunderstood verses in the Bible. It is one of the few verses that most unbelievers can quote perfectly. Sadly, because of poor pastoral teaching, most Christians do not do much better in their understanding than the unbeliever, who loves to quote it the moment someone suggests that he has done something wrong. In this passage, Jesus is not telling believers to mind their own business. He is warning them not to make judgments based on a man-made unbiblical standard. Paul also made a command concerning "not judging" in 1 Corinthians 4:5, where he says, "...do not go on passing judgment before the time, but wait until the Lord comes who will both bring to light the things hidden in the darkness and disclose the motives of men's hearts..." This verse makes a clear prohibition against Christians making judgments about the motives, which are behind a fellow believer's actions. Only God can look into a man's heart and know with assurance why anyone does what he does. Therefore, we are forbidden to make judgments about anyone's motives unless he chooses to divulge them.

But we must not stop there. Paul goes on in chapter five to discuss the sin of an incestuous man who was a member of the fellowship. He rebukes the Corinthians for not dealing with the problem, and then he asserts, "I ... have already judged him." Paul was certainly not making a judgment concerning the man's motives. However, he was affirming that because God had already made laws prohibiting this sinful behavior, his judgment was based upon God's Word. He was taking his stand with God, as he rebuked the Corinthian church for not doing the same. He then concludes the chapter by saying, "For what have I to do with judging outsiders? Do you not judge those who are within the church? But those who are outside, God judges. Remove the wicked man from among yourselves" (1 Cor 5:12-13). Paul's clear teaching is that God will judge the unbeliever, but it is the responsibility for Christians to judge one another by the standard of the Word of God. What God calls sin, we must call sin. Those who refuse to repent are eventually to be put out of the church, and the church is to have no fellowship or social interaction with them until they repent.

So back in Matthew 7:3-5, Jesus goes on to explain that before any confrontation of another brother can take place, each believer must first examine his own life to make sure that he himself is not just as, or even more, guilty as the one whom he is preparing to confront.

> Brethren, even if anyone is caught in any trespass, you who are spiritual, restore such a one in a spirit of gentleness; each one looking to yourself, so that you too will not be tempted. Bear one another's burdens, and thereby fulfill the law of Christ. (Galatians 6:1-2)

Continuing in the theme of Matthew 7, it is only when we have examined ourselves and repented of our own sins before God that we are spiritually fit and controlled tools for Him to use in the confrontation of another sinning brother. We are called not only to rebuke on the basis of sin, which is clearly defined in God's Word; we are also commanded to restore (*katartizo*). This is a medical term used to describe the setting or mending of a broken bone.[1] Metaphorically speaking, here is a member of the body of Christ that is hanging limp and useless because of his sin. We, who are fellow members of Christ's body, must endeavor to bring him to repentance and back into fellowship and active service in the body. When one member of the human body is hurting, the healthy parts help to bear the burden until it is well. And so it is, when it comes to the restoration of sinning Christians to fellowship with God and with each other. Just because a broken or dislocated bone is set does not mean that it is healed

---

[1] John MacArthur, Jr, MacArthur New Testament Commentary: Galatians (Chicago: Moody Press, 1987), 179.

and strong. We in Christ's body must be prepared to carry an extra load of care and prayer for this brother until he is spiritually strong enough to stand on his own.

In Matthew 18:15-17, Jesus provides the clearest step-by-step instruction of how we are to attempt the restoration of a sinning brother.

> If your brother sins, go and show him his fault in private; if he listens to you, you have won your brother. But if he does not listen to you, take one or two more with you, so that by the mouth of two or three witnesses every fact may be confirmed. If he refuses to listen to them, tell it to the church; and if he refuses to listen even to the church, let him be to you as a Gentile and a tax collector. (Matthew 18:15-17)

It is critical to point out that sin is biblically defined. Wearing a purple necktie with pink dots and orange stripes is certainly horrible fashion sense, but it is not sin. Once the Christian has gone through the aforementioned self-examination and personal repentance, then, and only then, is he fit to confront his brother with his sin in hopes of restoring him to fellowship with God and His people.

Throughout this process, those who must confront their sinning brethren must at the same time seek to provide truckloads of biblical hope. They must assure their brother that no matter what he has done, both God and the church will be eager to forgive and restore him to fellowship, lest he "... be overwhelmed by excessive sorrow" (2 Cor 2:7). The Matthew 18:15 passage clearly states that the confrontation must be done privately. It does not say, "Take ten of your friends and gang up on him." When this instruction is carefully followed, most church discipline will end here at step one, with the sinning brother understanding, confessing, and repenting of his sin. However, if he does not hear and repent, we must move on to step two, where the same procedure is repeated, but this time it is to be done in the presence of no more than one or two other people, who act as witnesses.

Although "The Matthew 18 Process" rarely gets this far, on those rare occasions that it does, it will usually end here with the confession, repentance, and restoration of the sinning brother. However, if he refuses to listen to the two or three of you, then we must move on to step three, where this man's sinning is to be revealed to the entire church. The elders in this case would need to make a careful investigation of the facts, to first ensure that this believer has actually sinned and that he refuses to repent. In the case of elders, Paul makes it clear in 1 Timothy 5:19 that they are to be shielded from the frivolous and/or malicious accusations of individuals, saying, "Do not receive an accusation against an elder except on the basis of two or three witnesses." The fact that he has already gone through such an intense biblical scrutiny prior to becoming an elder presupposes that his word should be believed over a single accuser.

Once the elders have done a full investigation and are convinced of the man's sin and stubbornness, they will then need to inform the entire church of his sin and willful refusal to repent. The church would then be exhorted to individually contact and urge him to repentance.

After steps one, two, and three have been carefully followed, and once the elders have again determined that he is still unrepentant, the church discipline process must move on to step four, where he is to be formally removed from the fellowship. It must be clearly understood that this action is not taking place because of his original sin that precipitated the process in the first place. He is being removed because of his stubborn refusal to confess and repent of it, which has the effect of piling sin upon sin. He is to be treated by the church as the Jews of the First Century treated the Gentiles and tax-gatherers of their day, meaning there is to be no social contact or fellowship with him (1 Cor 5:9-13). The only interaction would be to continue urging him to repent and be restored, which have been the goals all along. For sinning elders, who go through this process and continue to be unrepentant, Paul adds an extra point of discipline: "Those who continue in sin, rebuke in the presence of all, so that the rest also will be fearful of sinning" (1 Tim 5:20). In such a scenario, the message to the church as a whole and to the other serving elders is that no one, no matter how high his position of leadership in the church, will get away with unrepentant sinning. It is essential to point out here that if the excommunicated sinner eventually repents, then his restoration to the church fellowship must be as public as was his excommunication.

As has been stated earlier, disciplined church elders can always be restored to fellowship with Christ and His church. However, the church must be extremely careful concerning any restoration to eldership. Certain sins will only disqualify a repentant elder temporarily, while others will disqualify him permanently regardless of his repentance and restoration to the fellowship. Certain aforementioned sins permanently destroy the foundation of trust that a congregation must have in their pastors. Paul exhorted the entire Galatian church, "Do not be deceived, God is not mocked; for whatever a man sows, this he will also reap." (Gal 6:7). All Christians, not just pastors, would do well to remember that they cannot sow seeds to the flesh with the expectation of a crop failure.

CHAPTER 7

BIBLICAL TREATMENT OF DISQUALIFIED ELDERS

As has been previous demonstrated, not all sins are alike, and therefore, the treatment of repentant disqualified and/or disciplined repentant elders will not all be the same. Depending on the gravity of the disqualification, some men may in time be brought back into the elder ministry. For example, if a man has been disqualified because of his unruly children, this need not be a permanent disqualification. Through biblical counseling to help him with wise parenting, he could become requalified. Honorable men step down until the disqualifying issues in their lives and/or characters are rectified.

In cases of moral failure, such as adultery, restoration to the pastoral ministry is simply not an option. But if the man has shown himself to be repentant, there is no reason why in time he could not be allowed to serve the church as a layman. Both the scope and timing of his participation as a layman is entirely in the hands of his church elders, but they must have a clear assurance through the man's attitude of submission and the passing of time that he is, in fact, truly repentant. In such cases, the church is not guilty of "shooting its own wounded." We are merely seeking to remove fallen elders off the front lines of battle and into the hospital for treatment.

Sadly, a pastor who has been disciplined by the church for immorality often expects and even demands to be fully restored to the pastorate. In such cases, he typically refuses to submit to the church and the elders that disciplined him. He often harshly judges the disciplining body, accusing them of being unkind, unloving, and unforgiving, saying things like, "God loves and has forgiven me; what's the matter with you?" Such accusations are not only unbiblical and self-serving, but they reveal a prideful and selfish arrogance, which in itself demonstrates continued reason for biblical disqualification. Who are the wounded ones here? Certainly it is not him, except for the wounds he has brought upon himself. He is the one who has wounded his family, the church, and God's reputation in the community. Where was his love for God, his family, and his church when he was in the midst of his deceitful immorality? Idolatrous self-love was not only being demonstrated then, but it is still evident through his unbiblical expectations to be restored to the ministry.

This was the case with one pastor of international notoriety. Every church ministry in which he served for over thirty-five years flourished. Even though there were accusations brought against him, no one was ever able to get two or three corroborating witnesses in one place to initiate church discipline. After thirty-five years, he was finally found out beyond any shadow of doubt, and although he finally admitted to his most recent adultery, he would never specifically confess to any of the others. He would neither deny nor admit to any previous adulterous behaviors, saying only, "Well, I had some issues back then." As is so often the case, and much to my personal sadness, he refused to submit to any of the elders' demands concerning his spiritual restoration to God and to the church. He simply walked away, saying that he now had a whole new understanding and appreciation of the wonderful grace of God. Today, he still retains his title of Pastor, and he continues in his international ministry of speaking to missionaries and churches. It was to such prideful and arrogant men that Solomon wrote, "Pride goes before destruction, and a haughty spirit before stumbling" (Prov 16:18). The same God who cut down the proud Nebuchadnezzar like a tree, will one day deal with all such arrogance and pride.

In one sense, it is good for these men to look to King David's example after he repented of his adultery and murder. David never asked to remain on as king. Quite the contrary, he was humbly grateful to be restored to fellowship with his God. For him, that was enough. Because of David's "... broken and a contrite heart ..." (Ps 51:17), God allowed him not only to live but also to remain on as king. However, the stain of his sin and its impact on his family followed him to the grave. If a man is truly repentant, he will plead with God to restore and to protect his family from the ravages of his sin. He will make no demands on them or the church. And like David, shame and sorrow will likely follow him to his grave and beyond. The names of immoral men stink long after they are gone!

CONCLUSION

Paul encouraged Timothy, "It is a trustworthy statement: if any man aspires to the office of overseer, it is a fine work he desires to do" (1 Tim 3:1). Of all the blessings a man could receive, second only to having a godly wife and children, to be called by God to serve Him and His church as an elder must be the highest. The potentials for the glory and honor of God and the good of His people, or heartache and disgrace are in his own hands. Thankfully, there are a growing number of biblically-qualified God-fearing men who continue to stand firm as under-shepherds of God's flock, who look forward to hearing the words of our Lord saying, "Well done good and faithful servant ... enter into the joy of your Master" (Matt 25:21)

APPENDIX – A

Discipling of Elders and Those Who Would Seek to Become Elders

I. Using an exhaustive concordance or word study book, seek to determine the ways in which the following Greek words are translated into the *King James* and *New American Standard Versions* of the Bible.

Presbuteros

episkopos

poimen

diakonos

gune

II. Study the following passages to determine whether or not all these words are referring to the same church office. If not list them by major category.

1 Timothy 3:1-13

Titus 1:5-11

Ephesians 4:11-12

1 Timothy 5:17-22

2 John:1 and 3 John:1

1 Peter 5:1-4

Galatians 2:11-21

Hebrews 13:15

Acts 20:17, 28-31

III. Study the following passages of Scripture and list the biblical qualifications that must first be in place before a person can serve in the office of an elder. The purpose of this study is for the counselee to learn the high and demanding biblical qualifications that must be in place before one can be placed in the position as an elder. It will also help him to realize if his current elders are biblically qualified.

1 Timothy 3:1-13

Titus 1:5-11

Ephesians 4:11-12

1 Timothy 5:17-22

1 Peter 5:1-4

Galatians 2:11-21

Hebrews 13:15

Acts 20:17, 28-31

IV. Study the following passages and answer the questions. The purpose of this assignment is to assist the counselee in the clear biblical differences between elders and deacons concerning how they serve the church, how they come into office, and any chain of command that may exist between them.

    A. How were elders and deacons placed into office?

Titus 1:5

Acts 6:1-7

1 Timothy 5:22

1 Timothy 3:10

    B. What are the duties of a church elder?

1 Peter 5:3; Philippians 4:9

Acts 6:4

Titus 1:9 (3 duties)

Titus 1:10-11

Galatians 2:11-21

Ephesians 4:11-12

Acts 6:1-6; 1 Peter 5:2

Acts 6:3, 5-6

Acts 20:35

C. What is the main difference in qualification between a deacon and an elder?

D. What subordination is there between elders and deacons?

V. Study the following passages and carefully list out the biblical process and order for disqualifying an elder from his position. Once the list is made, consider from assignment #2 what kinds of sins would disqualify an elder or deacon permanently from service. The purpose for this assignment is for the counselee to learn what steps must be taken for the reproving and possible removing of an elder. Not only the steps are important, but also the manner and order in which they are taken.

Matthew 7:1-5; Galatians 6:1

Matthew 18:15-17

1 Timothy 5:19

1 Timothy 5:21

1 Timothy 5:20

1 Corinthians 5:5

VI. Answer the following questions. The purpose for this assignment is help the counselee understand what will happen if a church does not exercise church discipline and why unrepentant professing Christians must be treated so firmly.

   A. What dangers does the Bible present for not practicing church discipline?

   1 Corinthians 5:6

   Hebrews 3:13

   1 Timothy 3:7; 2 Corinthians 6:3

   B. How is the church to treat the officially disciplined and unrepentant church member or ex-elder? Are there any differences stated between regular members and elders?

   1 Timothy 5:20

   1 Corinthians 5:9-13

C. How are unrepentant professing Christians to be treated and why?

Matthew 18:15-17

1 Timothy 5:20

1 Corinthians 5:9-13

VII. Answer the following questions. The purpose of this assignment is to assist the counselee in understanding some of the practical reasons for the high biblical qualification for those who would lead and serve God's church.

A. Why must elders *desire* the office rather than being drafted or pressured into taking it? (1 Timothy 3:1)

B. Why would flirting or sexual sin disqualify a man from being an elder?

1 Timothy 3:2

Titus 1:6-7

C. Why is it important for elders to be hospitable? (1 Timothy 3:2)

D. Why could drinking disqualify an elder from service?

1 Timothy 3:3

1 Corinthians 8:1-13

E. Why is it important for elders to be *free from the love of money*? (1 Timothy 3:3)

F. Why does God place such high standards upon the elders who shepherd His church? (1 Timothy 3:4-5)

G. Why must elders and deacons not be hastily chosen or be new converts?

1 Timothy 3:6-7

1 Timothy 5:22

H. Why is it a logical conclusion that elders should have to measure up to all the moral qualifications that are required of deacons and deaconesses even if they are not specifically mentioned in the qualification lists for elders? (1 Timothy 3:8-13)

VIII. Answer the following questions. The purpose of this assignment is to assist the counselee in understanding some of the practical reasons for the high biblical qualification for those who would lead and serve God's church.

A. Why did God want elders appointed in every city where there was a church, rather than merely having regional elders? (Titus 1:5)

B. From the context, why does *"having children who believe"* not refer to young children? (Titus 1:6)

C. What problems would be caused by having an elder who was *quick tempered* or *pugnacious?* (Titus 1:7)

D. What problems could be caused by having an elder who was *fond of sordid gain*? (Titus 1:7)

E. Why is it important for an elder to *love what is good*? (Titus 1:8)

F. Why must elders be able to understand and teach the Word of God? (Titus 1:9-11)

IX. Answer the following questions. The purposes of this assignment are to correct unbiblical beliefs about judging the brethren and to make sure that the Christian understands the importance of self-examination and repentance before attempting to restore a sinning brother.

    A. What are Christians to *judge* and not to *judge*?

Matthew 7:1-5

1 Corinthians 4:5

1 Corinthians 5:5, 9-13

    B. What must a Christian do before he attempts to rebuke/restore his sinning brother?

Matthew 7:1-5

Galatians 6:1-2

X. The purpose of this assignment is to give the counselee some practical applications of the biblical principles learned through the aforementioned projects. Plan an interview with a long-standing elder of a large church to determine:

A. Do they follow the biblical qualifications for the appointment of elders?

B. Do they exercise church discipline, and if so, how?

C. What problems have they had when elders no longer meet the biblical qualifications?

D. What have they done when elders no longer meet the biblical qualifications?

E. Have they had elders who voluntarily stepped down from their positions because of nonpermanent or permanent biblical disqualifications?

F. Have any of these men who resigned come back on the board, and what were the ramifications?

G. How has God blessed the church for obedience or disciplined the church for disobedience in the matter of appointing and retaining elders?

H. What constitutional safeguards have they written in to protect the church from lawsuits for exercising church discipline?

XI. Make a list of the biblical qualifications for elders that you currently meet and another list of the qualifications that you do not currently meet. While continuing to nurture the qualified areas, determine what you can or must do in the unqualified areas for the purpose of Christian growth, whether or not you will ever serve as an elder. The purpose of this assignment is to make it clear that all the moral and theological qualifications should be the desire and quest of all Christians for God's glory and their sanctification.

APPENDIX – B

"To Drink or Not to Drink? — That is the Question"[1]

Looking back over 50 years since my conversion to Christ, and more than 40 years of ministry, there seems to be one question that comes up over-and-over again. Although it can be asked many ways, all of the questions can be boiled down to one: *"Is it OK for a Christian to drink alcoholic beverages?"* What may seem to be a simple question, turns out to not be so simple after all; because there is no single passage of scripture that gives us an answer one way or the other. But that should not dissuade or discourage even the inexperienced Bible student from doing a little digging. I would remind my readers that there is also no single passage of scripture that proves the "Trinity," either, and yet every credible Bible scholar for almost 2000 years has affirmed it to be a provable and foundational tenant of the Christian faith.

Everyone, who has ever sat under my teaching, will affirm that I am "allergic to legalism" in all of its ugly forms. Whether it is a legalism that pridefully affirms salvation by works, or a legalism that seeks Christian sanctification by the same motive and means, I hate them both. We would all do well to remember that Jesus reserved His strongest castigations and condemnations for the self-righteous Scribes, Pharisees, Priests, and Lawyers of His day, who were constantly engaged in making new laws to govern human behavior and worship, where God

---

[1] All rights reserved in all countries. Larry S. Nelson.

made no such laws. And unfortunately, they are still with us today, more and worse than ever!

And when it comes to the question of whether or not it is OK for a Christian to drink alcohol, I have heard many modern day legalists, who condemn the practice by twisting scripture to make their points. So in this short essay, I want to focus on just a few passages of scripture, which I hope will provide light, and not just heat, to this oft-argued question.

Furthermore, those of us who are getting up in years, can remember when the medical profession told us that butter was good for our health. But later they told us that it was bad, and that we should only eat margarine. But then they changed their minds again. Similarly, eggs were once good for us, and then they were bad, but now they are good again. The problem with even sincere and honest medical research is that these folks don't know what they don't know. But as new discoveries are made, past dogmatic warnings sometimes need to change in order to be true to the latest scientific findings. And so it is with the consumption of alcoholic beverages. In recent history, some researchers have touted what they believe to be the benefits of regular moderate alcohol consumption. But now there are conflicting studies which have concluded that no one should consume alcohol in any amount, ever. And who knows whether another study will come out in a few years to debunk the last one?

When it comes to smoking, I believe that the entire medical profession has conclusively proven that it is harmful to one's health, and I doubt that these conclusions will ever change. But even if all the researchers were to agree that the consumption of alcohol had some medicinal benefit, or conversely, that it was provably harmful to the body, I do not believe that medical research should be either the first or the final word on the matter for the Christian of any age or generation.

With all that said, I will tell you at the outset, I do not drink alcohol in any form, under any conditions, ever; and I have not done so since the earliest days of my Christian life. Now I wish I could report that my reasons for total abstinence have always been biblical, and that without any hint of legalism; but this is not the case. As a young Christian, without any input or help from others, my conviction was based upon passages such as:

> Do you not know that you are a temple of God and that the Spirit of God dwells in you? If any man destroys the temple of God, God will destroy him, for the temple of God is holy, and that is what you are. (1 Corinthians 3:16-17 NAS95)

I remember reasoning to myself, "Why are you pouring this poison into God's temple?" Unfortunately, at the time, I knew nothing about exegesis or hermeneutics, so I did not understand that I was both misinterpreting and misapplying the text.

At that same time, I was living in a college fraternity, where "barn keggers" happened regularly. I remember one night sitting on a bale of hay with a beer in one hand and my Bible in the other, as I tried to share my new Christian faith with one of my fraternity buddies, who wasted no time pointing out what he considered to be my own hypocrisy. And that was the day I stopped drinking.

Clearly, the misinterpretation of scripture and caving into the self-righteous criticisms of others make a very poor, and biblically undefendable, foundation for any Christian's behavior. But as I grew in my faith and the ability to unpack the whole of scripture, I not only learned that my aforementioned reasonings were faulty, but I also began to see that Jesus' summation of the Law had much to say about the question before us.

> "Teacher, which is the great commandment in the Law?" And He said to him, "YOU SHALL LOVE THE LORD YOUR GOD WITH ALL YOUR HEART, AND WITH ALL YOUR SOUL, AND WITH ALL YOUR MIND. This is the great and foremost commandment. The second is like it, YOU SHALL LOVE YOUR NEIGHBOR AS YOURSELF. On these two commandments depend the whole Law and the Prophets." (Matthew 22:36-40 NAS95)

The capital letters of the New American Standard Bible indicate that Jesus was quoting from the Old Testament books of: Deuteronomy 6:5; 10:12; 30:6 and Leviticus 19:18. And later, on the night before His crucifixion, He brought this Old Testament teaching into clear focus, declaring what would become the norm for all His followers from that time forward.

> A new commandment I give to you, that you love one another, even as I have loved you, that you also love one another. By this all men will know that you are My disciples, if you have love for one another. (John 13:34-35 NAS95)

And Peter would later exhort his readers to sincerely and fervently love one another.

> Since you have in obedience to the truth purified your souls for a sincere love of the brethren, fervently love one another from the heart. (1 Peter 1:22 NAS95)

The Apostle John even intensified, Jesus' command by declaring that love for our brethren is one of the clearest tests of genuine Christian faith.

> Beloved, let us love one another, for love is from God; and everyone who loves is born of God and knows God. The one who does not love does not know God, for God is love. (1 John 4:7-8 NAS95)

By now you should be asking, "Of course, we are supposed to love one another, but what does that have to do with whether or not it is OK for Christians to drink?" Simply put, I believe that our love for our brothers and sisters in Christ has everything to do with it. In fact, Paul taught that love for our brethren should be at the very heart of all principles and motives for determining our actions in the Christian life. Paul referenced a Corinthian proverb saying,

> "All things are lawful for me, but not all things are profitable. All things are lawful for me, but I will not be mastered by anything." (1 Corinthians 6:12 NAS95)

For thousands of years, no sensible person, medical or otherwise, would disagree with the potential addictiveness of alcoholic beverages. Almost everyone has personal first-hand knowledge of individuals, entire families, and even cultures that have been devastated by addiction to alcohol. And even though there is no absolute biblical prohibition, no one can deny that millions have been, "mastered" by it. I doubt that anyone starts to drink with the intention of having alcohol become their master, and no one can know ahead of time whether or not it will happen to them. But the potential is always there.

Allow me to drill down into this point just a little deeper. Most people who drink in moderation say things like, "I never get drunk; this just helps me to relax after a tough day at work," or, "A couple of drinks help me to loosen up so that I am not so nervous in social settings." Please take notice of Paul's command to the church at Ephesus.

> Therefore be careful how you walk, not as unwise men but as wise, making the most of your time, because the days are evil. So then do not be foolish, but understand what the will of the Lord is. And do not get drunk with wine, for that is dissipation, but be filled with the Spirit,... (Ephesians 5:15-18 NAS95)

Even for those who never get drunk, Paul is exhorting every Christian to careful and wise living, where we are to make the most of our time. The word "filled," as it is used here in the Greek, has nothing to do with volume. It means "to control." So the best Greek rendering of verse 18 would go like this: "Do not let wine control you ... but be being constantly controlled by the Holy Spirit." Obviously, drunkenness is forbidden here, but it is also speaking to the one who wants a drink to relax, or to be less nervous, or to be more social. Simply put, if you need a drink to relax, or to calm your nerves, or to be social, then you are relying on something other than the controlling power of the indwelling Holy Spirit. Notice how Paul describes the one who is living under the control of the Holy Spirit.

> But the fruit of the Spirit is love, joy, peace, patience, kindness, goodness, faithfulness, gentleness, self-control; against such things there is no law. (Galatians 5:22-23 NAS95)

Simply put, Christians do not need to drink alcohol in order to relax or to be social. These graces are promised to the Holy Spirit-controlled Christian, who has no need to produce them artificially through drinking alcohol, which now brings me to the heart of the question. Please note again that Paul declares, "... the fruit of the Spirit is love ..."

As we have seen previously, for Christians, love for God and others should be at the heart of all our behaviors. Apparently, the church at Corinth had posed a question to the Apostle Paul concerning whether or not it was OK for a Christian to eat meat that had been sacrificed to idols. The ancient city of Corinth was filled with temples that were devoted to the worship of false gods. This "worship" included the sacrifice of animals, drunkenness, and cult prostitution. Apparently, there must have been a surplus, so they set up a meat market in the back, where people could buy what was likely the best meat in town at a bargain price. Hence the question: "Is it OK for Christians to eat meat that has been sacrificed to idols?"

> Therefore concerning the eating of things sacrificed to idols, we know that there is no such thing as an idol in the world, and that there is no God but one. For even if there are so-called gods whether in heaven or on earth, as indeed there are many gods and many lords, yet for us there is but one God, the Father, from whom are all things and we exist for Him; and one Lord, Jesus Christ, by whom are all things, and we exist through Him. However not all men have this knowledge; but some, being accustomed to the idol until now, eat food as if it were sacrificed to an idol; and their conscience being weak is defiled. But food will not commend us to God; we are neither the worse if we do not eat, nor the better if we do eat. But take care that this liberty of yours does not somehow become a stumbling block to the weak. For if someone sees you, who have knowledge, dining in an idol's temple, will not his conscience, if he is weak, be

strengthened to eat things sacrificed to idols? For through your knowledge he who is weak is ruined, the brother for whose sake Christ died. And so, by sinning against the brethren and wounding their conscience when it is weak, you sin against Christ. Therefore, if food causes my brother to stumble, I will never eat meat again, so that I will not cause my brother to stumble. (1 Corinthians 8:4-13 NAS95)

Paul makes it clear that the meat was unaffected, even though it had been sacrificed to idols, by saying, "But food will not commend us to God; we are neither the worse if we do not eat, nor the better if we do eat" (:13). It is safe to say that virtually all of the first Christians in Corinth were accustomed to idol worship and the debauchery that went along with it. And so Paul quickly moves to the heart of the matter. Far more important than the actual meat, which was no issue at all, was the danger that every Christian needed to pay close attention to. Paul warns, "But take care that this liberty of yours does not somehow become a stumbling block to the weak" (:9). In the next verses, Paul paints a picture of a strong mature Christian, who is able to eat his steak right there in the temple, and not even be tempted by the idolatry and debauchery surrounding him. But then he adds a weaker brother to the picture, who sees this mature Christian eating, and he says to himself, "I am a Christian too, and if he can do it, I can do it!"

But this weaker brother is tempted by all the debauchery to return to his previous idolatrous life, and he falls into sin; and Paul lays the blame at the stronger brother's feet, saying, "For through your knowledge he who is weak is ruined, the brother for whose sake Christ died. And so, by sinning against the brethren and wounding their conscience when it is weak, you sin against Christ" (11:12). Then Paul makes it very personal, by declaring, "Therefore, if food causes my brother to stumble, I will never eat meat again, so that I will not cause my brother to stumble" (:13). Obviously, Paul did not become a vegetarian. He was merely stating in very strong terms that it was not his personal liberty and/or right to eat this meat that was at issue here. The important thing for him, and for all of us, is that we should be willing to limit our liberty and/or personal rights, in order to protect a weaker brother from stumbling into sin by following our example.

The entire chapter of Romans 14 is devoted to this very subject, which begins with Paul referring to those who are weak and others who are strong in the faith. Next he commands, "Therefore let us ... determine this--not to put an obstacle or a stumbling block in a brother's way" (:13). And then he says, "For if because of food your brother is hurt, you are no longer walking according to love. Do not destroy with your food him for whom Christ died" (:15). Whether we like it or not, it is a fact that those who are younger and/or weaker in the faith are looking at the examples we set for them. Notice how Paul broadens the practical application of his discussion and instruction by adding another important word, which speaks directly to the question at hand.

> Therefore do not let what is for you a good thing be spoken of as evil; for the kingdom of God is not eating and **drinking**, but righteousness and peace and joy in the Holy Spirit. (Romans 14:16-17 NAS95)

In contrast to the potential of putting "an obstacle or a stumbling block in a brother's way" (:13), Paul now declares:

> For he who in this way serves Christ is acceptable to God and approved by men. So then let us pursue the things which make for peace and the building up of one another. (Romans 14:18-19 NAS95)

The issue is not my own personal rights, or what I can get away with. It is how much do I love my weaker brother? How much do I want to see him built up in his faith? And which of my personal rights am I willing to give up in order to keep from putting a stumbling block in his way? This matter has nothing to do with <u>legalism</u>, but it has everything to do with <u>love</u>! If we truly love our weaker brothers and sisters in Christ, then we will be careful to set the kind of example that does not tempt them to fall into sin.

Paul's warnings and exhortations just keep getting stronger as he commands:

> Do not tear down the work of God for the sake of food. All things indeed are clean, but they are evil for the man who eats and gives offense. 21 It is good not to eat meat or to **<u>drink wine</u>**, or to do **<u>anything</u>** by which your brother stumbles. (Romans 14:20-21 NAS95)

Even as Paul was able to eat meat that had been sacrificed to idols, without any negative effects to his soul or body, you too may be able to drink alcohol in moderation without any harmful effects. But mature Christians understand that none of us lives for himself. After Cain murdered his brother, Abel, God said to Cain, "Where is Abel your brother?" And he said, "I do not know. Am I my brother's keeper?" (Genesis 4:9). The obvious, and yet unspoken, answer was, **"Yes, you are your brother's keeper!"**

This fact alone should provide emphasis to the final words of Romans 14 where Paul says:

> The faith which you have, have as your own conviction before God. Happy is he who does not condemn himself in what he approves. But he who doubts is condemned if he eats, because his eating is not from faith; and whatever is not from faith is sin. (Romans 14:22-23 NAS95)

In light of these scriptures, I do not understand how any mature Christian, who has any understanding of the potential enslaving dangers of alcohol abuse, can drink it in any form, and say that he is doing so from faith without any doubts of how this will possibly affect those who are looking on. Again, please understand that my stated concerns and convictions have nothing to do with <u>legalism</u>, but everything to do with <u>love</u> for those who are looking up to me and the examples I set for them.

I believe that 1 Corinthians 10:31 provides us with a clear summary of the Christian life. "Whether, then, you eat or drink or whatever you do, do all to the glory of God." This command lays out a very high standard for every Christian. The conclusions of this essay have primarily focused on how a mature Christian's behavior might negatively affect a weaker brother, and thereby lead him into sin. However, the context of this verse includes even those who are outside the church.

> Give no offense either to Jews or to Greeks or to the church of God; just as I also please all men in all things, not seeking my own profit but the profit of the many, so that they may be saved. (1 Corinthians 10:32-33 NAS95)

For any who would still see total abstinence as just another form of "legalism," please consider Paul's admonition to Timothy, who was the pastor of the church at Ephesus.

> No longer drink water exclusively, but use a little wine for the sake of your stomach and your frequent ailments. (1 Timothy 5:23 NAS95)

While we take pure water for granted, the ancient writers of the Talmud, Hippocrates, Pliny, and Plutarch, all spoke of the of the medicinal effects of wine to prevent stomach problems believed to be caused by polluted water (*The MacArthur New Testament Commentary: 1 Timothy*, p. 225). Even though they knew nothing about bacterial microbes or dysentery, it had been discovered that just adding a little wine to the household water jar, would usually prevent stomach ailments. But in spite of this well known problem, and common practice, this text makes it clear that Timothy had made the choice to totally abstain from wine. In the Greek, Paul uses the "Imperative Mood" twice in one sentence. This means that he was not just making suggestions; these were commands. Although we are not told why Timothy was a total abstainer, it is reasonable to believe that Paul's previously stated concerns about causing weaker brothers to stumble would have likely influenced his decision.

So as you consider, "Is it OK for a Christian to drink Alcoholic beverages?" I will conclude with one final exhortation from the Apostle Paul, which must govern all of our behaviors.

> Do nothing from selfishness or empty conceit, but with humility of mind regard one another as more important than yourselves; 4 do not merely look out for your own personal interests, but also for the interests of others. (Philippians 2:3-4 NAS95)

BIBLIOGRAPHY

Adams, Jay. *Handbook of Church Discipline.* Grand Rapids: Zondervan Publishing House, 1986.

Armstrong, John. *The Stain that Stays: The Church's Response to the Sexual Misconduct of its Leaders*. Fearn, Ross-shire: Christian Focus Publications, 2000.

Baker, Don. *Beyond Forgiveness*. Portland: Multnomah Press, 1984.

Baxter, Richard. *The Reformed Pastor*. London: Banner of Truth, 1983.

Beck, James R. and Bloomberg, Craig L. *Two Views on Women in Ministry*. Grand Rapids: Zondervan Publishing House, 2001.

Belcher, Richard P. *A Journey in Authority*. Colombia: Richbarry Press, 1996.

Belleville, Linda L. *Women Leaders and the Church.* Grand Rapids, Baker Books, 1999.

Bridges, Charles. *The Christian Ministry with an Inquiry into the Causes of its Inefficiency.* Carlisle: Banner of Truth, 2001.

Clouse, Bonnidell and Robert (Editors). *Women in Ministry.* Downers Grove: Intervarsity Press, 1989.

Greenleaf, Robert. *Servant Leadership: A Journey Into the Nature of Legitimate Power and Greatness*. New York: Paulist Press, 1977.

Harrison, Everett. *Baker's Dictionary of Theology.* Grand Rapids: Baker Book House, 1960.

Hayford, Jack W. *Restoring Fallen Leaders.* Ventura: Regal Books, 1988.

House, H. Wayne. *The Role of Women in Ministry Today.* Nashville: Thomas Nelson, 1990.

Howard, Phillip Allen. *The Recognition and Training of Elders in the Local Church.* Dallas: Dallas Theological Seminary, 1986.

Hughes, Kent and Barbara. *Liberating Ministry from the Success Syndrome.* Wheaton: Tyndale House Publishers, Inc., 1987.

Keller, Philip. *A Shepherd Looks at the 23rd Psalm.* Grand Rapids: Zondervan Publishing House, 1970.

Knight, George W. III. *The Pastoral Epistles: A Commentary on the Greek Text.* Grand Rapids: William B. Eerdmans Publishing Company, 1992.

Ladd, George Eldon. *A Theology of the New Testament.* Grand Rapids: William B. Eerdmans Publishing Company, 1974.

Laney, J. Carl. *A Guide to Church Discipline.* Minneapolis: Bethany House, 1985.

Lindner, Phil. *Power Bible CD Version 3.3.* Bronson: Online Publishing Inc., 2001.

Lutzer, Erwin. *Pastor to Pastor.* Grand Rapids: Kregal Publications, 1998.

Lloyd-Jones, D. Martin. *Preaching and Preachers.* Grand Rapids: Zondervan Publishing House, 1971.

Lloyd-Jones, D. Martin. *Studies in the Sermon on the Mount.* Grand Rapids: William B. Eerdmans Publishing Company, 1984.

MacArthur, John F. *Answering Questions About Elders.* Panorama City: Grace to You, 1988.

The MacArthur New Testament Commentary: Acts 13-28 Chicago: Moody Press, 1996.

The MacArthur New Testament Commentary: 1 Corinthians. Chicago: Moody Press, 1984.

The MacArthur New Testament Commentary: Ephesians. Chicago: Moody Press, 1986.

The MacArthur New Testament Commentary: Galatians. Chicago: Moody Press, 1997.

The MacArthur New Testament Commentary: Hebrews. Chicago: Moody Press, 1983.

The MacArthur New Testament Commentary: Titus. Chicago: Moody Press, 1996.

The MacArthur New Testament Commentary: 1 Timothy. Chicago: Moody Press, 1995.

Malins, Joseph. *The Best Loved Poems of the American People*, editor: Hazel Felleman. New York: Doubleday, 1936.

Schaeffer, Francis A. *The Church at the End of the 20th Century.* Downers Grove: InterVarsity Press, 1970.

Spurgeon, Charles H. *Lectures to My Students.* Grand Rapids: Zondervan Publishing House, 1954.

Strauch, Alexander. *Biblical Eldership: An Urgent Call to Restore Biblical Church Leadership.* Littleton: Lewis and Roth Publishers, 1995.

Strauch, Alexander. *They Keep Watch Over Your Souls: 8 Sermons on Biblical Eldership (Cassette Tape Series).* Littleton: Lewis and Roth Publishers.

Wiersbe, Warren. *The Bible Exposition Commentary, Vol 2.* Wheaton: Victor Books, 1989.

Zuck, Roy B. (General Editor). *Vital Church Issues: Examining Principles and Practices in Church Leadership.* Grand Rapids: Kregal Publications, 1998.

About the Author

Larry Nelson is an expository Bible teaching pastor, who has been in ministry for 45 years. He has his Master's Degree in Biblical Counseling (MABC) from The Master's University, and he is a longstanding member of The Association of Certified Biblical Counselors - ACBC, previously known as The National Association of Nouthetic Counselors (NANC). Larry and his beloved wife, Marian, have been married for almost 50 years, and they are blessed with 4 believing children, and 9 grandchildren. He may be contacted at: askpastornelson@gmail.com

Made in the USA
Columbia, SC
19 April 2022